650.072

16

For RENEWAL
TEL: 01757 211017

This book is due for return on or before the last date shown below.

CONDUCTING

IN

for BUSINESS STUDENTS

D1440573

SAGE was founded in 1965 by Sara Miller McCune to support the dissemination of usable knowledge by publishing innovative and high-quality research and teaching content. Today, we publish more than 750 journals, including those of more than 300 learned societies, more than 800 new books per year, and a growing range of library products including archives, data, case studies, reports, conference highlights, and video. SAGE remains majority-owned by our founder, and after Sara's lifetime will become owned by a charitable trust that secures our continued independence.

Los Angeles | London | Washington DC | New Delhi | Singapore

CONDUCTING RESEARCH INTERVIEWS

for BUSINESS and MANAGEMENT STUDENTS

CATHERINE CASSELL

Los Angeles | London | New Delhi
Singapore | Washington DC

Los Angeles | London | New Delhi
Singapore | Washington DC

SAGE Publications Ltd
1 Oliver's Yard
55 City Road
London EC1Y 1SP

SAGE Publications Inc.
2455 Teller Road
Thousand Oaks, California 91320

SAGE Publications India Pvt Ltd
B 1/I 1 Mohan Cooperative Industrial Area
Mathura Road
New Delhi 110 044

SAGE Publications Asia-Pacific Pte Ltd
3 Church Street
#10-04 Samsung Hub
Singapore 049483

Editor: Kirsty Smy
Assistant editor: Nina Smith
Production editor: Sarah Cooke
Copyeditor: Sharon Cawood
Proofreader: Lynda Watson
Indexer: Judith Lavender
Marketing manager: Catherine Slinn
Cover designer: Francis Kenney
Typeset by: C&M Digitals (P) Ltd, Chennai, India
Printed and bound by CPI Group (UK) Ltd,
Croydon, CR0 4YY

© Catherine Cassell 2015

First published 2015

Apart from any fair dealing for the purposes of research or
private study, or criticism or review, as permitted under the
Copyright, Designs and Patents Act, 1988, this publication
may be reproduced, stored or transmitted in any form, or by
any means, only with the prior permission in writing of the
publishers, or in the case of reprographic reproduction,
in accordance with the terms of licences issued by the
Copyright Licensing Agency. Enquiries concerning
reproduction outside those terms should be sent to
the publishers.

Library of Congress Control Number: 2014943646

British Library Cataloguing in Publication data

A catalogue record for this book is available from
the British Library

MIX
Paper from
responsible sources
FSC   FSC® C013604
www.fsc.org

ISBN 978-1-44627-354-8
ISBN 978-1-44627-355-5 (pbk)

At SAGE we take sustainability seriously. Most of our products are printed in the UK using FSC papers and boards.
When we print overseas we ensure sustainable papers are used as measured by the Egmont grading system.
We undertake an annual audit to monitor our sustainability.

NEW SERIES FROM SAGE! MASTERING BUSINESS RESEARCH METHODS!

Providing practical guidance on using specific methods of data collection and data analysis, this series includes:

978-1-4462-7355-5

978-1-4462-7357-9

978-1-4462-7353-1

978-1-4462-7417-0

COMING SOON

Analysing Quantitative Data Using Classical Test Theory for Business and Management Students

Jeremy Dawson

978-1-4739-0751-5

Template Analysis for Business and Management Students

Nigel King, Joanna M. Brooks

978-1-4739-1157-4

Series Editors: Bill Lee, Mark N. K. Saunders and Vadake K. Narayanan

CONTENTS

EDITORS' INTRODUCTION TO THE *MASTERING BUSINESS RESEARCH METHODS* SERIES

Welcome to the *Mastering Business Research Methods* series. In recent years, there has been a great increase in the numbers of students reading masters level degrees across the business and management disciplines. A great number of these students have to prepare a dissertation towards the end of their degree programme in a time-frame of three to four months. For many students, this takes place after their taught modules have finished and is expected to be an independent piece of work. Whilst each student is supported in their dissertation or research project by an academic supervisor, the student will need to find out more detailed information about the method that he or she intends to use. Before starting their dissertations or research projects these students have usually been provided with little more than an overview across a wide range of methods as preparation for this often daunting task. If you are one such student, you are not alone. As university professors with a deep interest in research methods, we have provided this series of books to help students like you. Each book provides detailed information about a particular method to support you in your dissertation. We understand both what is involved in masters level dissertations, and what help students need with regard to methods in order to excel when writing a dissertation. This series is the only one that is designed with the specific objective of helping masters level students to undertake and prepare their dissertations.

Each book in our series is designed to provide sufficient knowledge about either a method of data collection or a method of data analysis, and each book is intended to be read by the student when undertaking particular stages of the research process, such as data collection or analysis. Each book is written in a clear way by highly respected authors who have considerable experience of teaching and writing about research methods. To help students find their way around each book, we have utilized a standard format, with each book having been organized into six chapters:

- **Chapter 1** introduces the method, considers how the method emerged for what purposes, and provides an outline of the remainder of the book.
- **Chapter 2** addresses the underlying philosophical assumptions that inform the uses of particular methods.
- **Chapter 3** discusses the components of the relevant method.
- **Chapter 4** considers the way in which the different components may be organized to use the method.
- **Chapter 5** provides examples of published studies that have used the method.
- **Chapter 6** concludes by reflecting on the strengths and weaknesses of that method.

We hope that reading your chosen books helps you in your dissertation.

Bill Lee, Mark NK Saunders and VK Narayanan

ABOUT THE SERIES EDITORS

Bill Lee, PhD is Professor of Accounting and Head of the Accounting and Financial Management Division at the University of Sheffield, UK. He has a long-standing interest in research methods and practice, in addition to his research into accounting and accountability issues. Bill's research has been published widely, including in: *Accounting Forum*; *British Accounting Review*; *Critical Perspectives on Accounting*; *Management Accounting Research*; *Omega*; and *Work, Employment & Society*. His publications in the area of research methods and practice include the co-edited collections *The Real Life Guide to Accounting Research* and *Challenges and Controversies in Management Research*.

Mark NK Saunders BA MSc PGCE PhD FCIPD is Professor of Business Research Methods in the Business School at the University of Surrey, UK. His research interests are research methods, in particular methods for understanding intra organisational relationships; human resource aspects of the management of change, in particular trust within and between organisations; and small and medium-sized enterprises. Mark's research has been published in journals including *Journal of Small Business Management*, *Field Methods*, *Human Relations*, *Management Learning* and *Social Science and Medicine*. He has co-authored and co-edited a range of books including *Research Methods for Business Students* (currently in its sixth edition) and the *Handbook of Research Methods on Trust*.

VK Narayanan is the Associate Dean for Research, Director of the Center for Research Excellence, and the Deloitte Touché Stubbs Professor of Strategy and Entrepreneurship in Drexel University, Philadelphia, PA. His articles have appeared in leading professional journals such as *Academy of Management Journal*, *Academy of Management Review*, *Accounting Organizations and Society*, *Journal of Applied Psychology*, *Journal of Management*, *Journal of Management Studies*, *Management Information Systems Quarterly*, *R&D Management* and *Strategic Management Journal*. Narayanan holds a bachelor's degree in mechanical engineering from the Indian Institute of Technology, Madras, a post graduate degree in business administration from the Indian Institute of Management, Ahmedabad, and a Ph.D. in business from the Graduate School of Business at the University of Pittsburgh, Pennsylvania.

ABOUT THE AUTHOR

Catherine Cassell has a longstanding interest in research methodology and the use of qualitative methods in the business, organization and management fields. She has co-edited four books for Sage – together with Gillian Symon – on qualitative organizational research and published numerous papers about the uses of qualitative research in the organizational psychology and management field more generally. She is also currently working as lead editor for the *Sage Handbook of Business and Management Qualitative Research Methods*. Catherine was the founding chair of British Academy of Management's Special Interest group in Research Methodology – a group she is still heavily involved with – and a founding member of the steering committee of the European Academy of Management's Special Interest Group in Research Methods and Research Practice. She is inaugural co-Editor of *Qualitative Research in Organizations and Management: an international journal*, and on the editorial boards of numerous other journals. She is a Fellow of the British Academy of Management and an Academic Fellow of the Chartered Institute of Personnel and Development.

Having previously held a number of senior academic appointments, she is currently Deputy Dean and Professor of Organizational Psychology at Leeds University Business School.

ACKNOWLEDGEMENTS

This book has been inspired by the numerous colleagues and students I have had the joy to discuss qualitative research with over the years. Thank you all for your interest and insights. It has been a real pleasure. And thanks especially to Gillian, my partner in crime and good friend for so long.

I have also had the privilege to work with a great team at Sage over a number of projects so thanks to them for always being interested in research methods and making things happen.

Finally, thank you as ever to Bill for all his support, affection and wise words. And to Matt, Danny and Caitlin, who although now pretty big, keep me just as pre-occupied and entertained as ever.

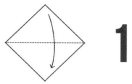

1

INTRODUCTION

INTRODUCTION

The interview is a popular technique within social sciences research. In the interview we have a method that can be used with different levels of structure; in a range of epistemological traditions; and which produces data that can be analysed in a variety of different ways. Hence, the interview is attractive to business, management and organizational researchers because of its variety and flexibility. Furthermore, the term interview is a familiar one, so potential interviewees will know what to expect when we ask if they are prepared to take part in an interview. It is important to state right at the outset that the research interview is somewhat different from other interviews we may encounter, such as selection interviews or other interviews in our social lives more generally. Rather, the research interview is a conversation where the researcher seeks information from an individual or group with the aim of using that information in order to progress their research. Therefore, one key difference of the research interview is that it is conducted as part of a research project and must produce data that can be analysed appropriately to come to some conclusions regarding a research question or area of interest.

The aim of this book is to provide an accessible guide to how to conduct interviews as part of a management, organization or business graduate-level research project, and throughout the book I use those domain terms interchangeably. The book covers a range of different interview types including structured, semi-structured and unstructured interviews. The assumption is that the interview data collected will form the empirical base of a tightly time-bound graduate research dissertation. In this introductory chapter, a brief history of the interview in organizational and management research is provided. We then consider the role of the interview and how it can be used; explore the kind of data that can be collected from an interview; and outline the approach taken to interviews and interviewing in the book overall.

HISTORY OF THE INTERVIEW

The interview has had a long history within the field of business and management research. Fontana and Frey (2005: 699) suggest that the development of interviewing in the twentieth century emerged from two major trends within the social sciences. The first was the need to gain a 'quality of responses' in the areas of counselling and clinical diagnosis, and the second was the increased concern with using interviews as the basis for psychological testing and management, a trend that emerged during the First World War. Perhaps the first classic study within the organizational field to rely on interviews was the Hawthorne Studies: a series of experiments conducted at the Western Electric company's Hawthorne works outside Chicago between 1924 and 1932. The focus of the experiments was on the different factors that impacted on the production levels of workers working in groups (Mayo, 1945). These studies were part of what came to be known as the Human Relations movement. Hollway (1991) suggests that interviewing as a qualitative data collection technique became prevalent around the same time as the human relations movement, because at this time within organization behaviour there was a move away from scientific management approaches where the worker was seen as cog in a machine, to a focus on the worker as an emotional human being. Interviews were seen as a valid way of collecting reliable and objective measurement data about the subjective aspects of worker experience, previously unacknowledged in the research of the time. The Second World War again saw an increase in the use of interviews both underpinning the development of psychological measurement (Hollway, 1991) and the documentation of the mental and emotional lives of soldiers (Fontana and Frey, 2005). In parallel developments, interviews were also being used as components of some of the classic ethnographic studies that underpinned the development of the organizational and management field. Examples include Jahoda, Lazarsfeld and Zeisel's (1972) intensive study of an unemployed community, Marienthal; Melvin Dalton's (1959) classic work of managerial practice, *Men who manage*; and *Working for Ford* (Benyon, 1973). These all drew on interview data as well as on a range of other data collection techniques.

By the 1970s and 1980s, interviews had become common place in social science research, and were evident in published work in the organizational and management field. During this period, different interpretations of the interview, according to the underlying epistemological stance, began to emerge. The increasing focus on new paradigms, and not least the linguistic turn that emerged in the 1980s, led to a range of new critiques of the interview and how it was used in organizational research. A particular challenge emerged from the critique that the interview was an 'active' process (e.g. Holstein and Gubrium, 1995) and could not be seen as a context-free occurrence or an isolated one-off event. These epistemological developments led to the variety of interview types we see today where the interview is used extensively in business, organizational and management research, and can be used to collect data in a variety of ways.

A cursory look at any of the main journals in the business and management field will highlight a variety of studies where interviews have been used. For example, in the first issue of the *British Journal of Management* published in 2014, three of the studies reported in the papers published drew on interview data. These were Bondy and Starkey's (2014) study of multinational companies and CSR; Kelan and Mah's (2014) study on gendered identification and MBA students; and Mallett and Wapshott's (2014) study of the use of humour in SMEs. As well as being extensively used in business and management research, organizations also make use of interviews, hence the ubiquity of the interview today.

TYPES OF DATA COLLECTED

It is possible to collect both qualitative and quantitative data in an interview though it is typically thought of as a technique for qualitative data collection. The type of data collected should link in with the research question that the researcher is seeking to answer and the analysis that is planned for that data. By quantitative data, we are referring here to the use of numerical scales, for example to assess people's attitudes or views. The use of quantitative methods tends to accompany a positivist paradigmatic stance. Here, the concern is with hypothesis testing and systematically measuring and analysing the relationships between variables through the use of statistics. Therefore, a key aim of quantitative methodological approaches is to conduct objective and replicable research. The procedures for conducting interview research from this perspective are therefore fairly standardized. So, for instance, as part of an interview, we could ask the interviewees to mark on a scale from 1 to 5 their views about a new product recently launched on to the market. This approach effectively means that the interviewee is completing the interviewer's questionnaire in the interview and is a strategy often used by telephone marketeers. This generation of quantitative data can be combined with qualitative, more open-ended questions too.

In terms of qualitative data, there are many different types of qualitative data and qualitative methods can be used in a range of philosophical traditions (Duberley et al., 2012). By qualitative data, we are referring here to non-numerical, textual or visual data where the focus is on the subjective understanding, meaning or sense-making processes of people or groups. Qualitative researchers are interested in understanding these experiences within the appropriate context or seeking what has been described as an insider view or account. Hence, the interview is particularly well-suited to the gathering of qualitative data. Qualitative methods are also more flexible in that we can focus on emerging themes during the research process (Cassell and Symon, 2004). So in an interview, for example, if the interviewee raises an interesting issue that we had not previously thought of and included in the interview schedule, we can follow that up and ask them more about it. The qualitative data produced can be quite diverse, depending on the type of interview used. For example, in life history method (see Musson, 2004) the interviewer can ask questions about the life of an individual to gain data regarding what experiences influence how they understand a given phenomena such as social class or gender in the workplace, whereas with critical incident technique (Flanagan, 1954) we may ask about specific events in the workplace to see how they are understood. Additionally, it may be that a researcher is interested in collecting qualitative and quantitative data at the same time. This is appropriate if the researcher's aim is to identify a statistically significant pattern across a given data set which can be enabled by quantitative analysis, yet also to access a more in-depth understanding of a particular phenomenon for which qualitative analysis is required.

Hence, the flexibility of the interview enables us to collect either qualitative and quantitative data, or a combination of both. Given that in the majority of cases interviews are used as a way of accessing qualitative data, this will be the major focus of this book.

THE ROLE OF THE INTERVIEW IN RESEARCH DESIGN

The interview can be used for a range of different purposes, depending on the research question and scope of the research. In examining the different roles that the interview can have in a research design, once again we find that there is considerable flexibility. For example, interviews can be used to explore a particular phenomenon – an exploratory interview – or can be used to clarify data derived from other sources in a confirmatory way. Here, we identify how interviews can be used in different ways as part of a research design: as part of a single method design; as part of a mixed methods design; and as part of a multi-method design. In some cases, depending on the research question, a graduate dissertation can be comprised of a series of interviews only, as a single method study design. A set of qualitative interviews in itself can provide a rich enough data set – see Box 1.1.

1.1   Using interviews in a research design based on interviews only

Jane is studying for a Masters in Human Resource Management. For her dissertation project, Jane wants to find out how men experience first-time fatherhood and the impact this has on their experiences in the workplace. From her literature review, Jane has discovered that there is little research about fathers in the workplace and how they manage their work–life balance after fatherhood, whereas there is a lot written about women returning to work after their first child. Given the little research in the field and her focus on individual experiences, Jane decides to base her research on a series of exploratory interviews with men who have become fathers in the last six months. Jane conducts in-depth interviews with 10 new fathers for her dissertation project.

The interview can also have a role in a mixed methods design project. Here, mixed methods refer to where qualitative and quantitative methods are used together. Hammersley (1996) characterizes three approaches to mixed methods research: triangulation, facilitation and complementarity. Interviews can be used in each of these approaches. Saunders, Lewis and Thornhill (2012: 683) define triangulation as 'The use of two or more independent sources of data or data collection methods within one study in order to help ensure that the data are telling you what you think they are telling you'. So, a study could involve conducting interviews and using a questionnaire to answer a given research question. In triangulating the findings from the two methods, the researcher would be looking for some consistency. In the facilitation approach, qualitative research can facilitate quantitative research through providing hypotheses - for example, a researcher could conduct a few interviews with key stakeholders in an organization to garner their views of a change process and use those findings to design a questionnaire to survey the views of all members of the organization. In terms of complementarity, quantitative research can lead to qualitative research, for example through enabling the selection of interviewees or in filling in the gaps (Bryman and Bell, 2007: 649). So, we could start by surveying the views of the whole organization, and, through an analysis of the findings, seek out some interviewees who can elaborate on those findings in more detail. An example is provided in Box 1.2.

1.2   Using interviews in a mixed methods design

Samir is studying for a Masters degree in Marketing and Customer Relationship Management. He is particularly interested in customer loyalty schemes and how small and medium-sized enterprises (SMEs) can potentially use such schemes to

(Continued)

(Continued)

ensure customer loyalty. In considering the methods he wants to use for his research dissertation, he is keen to use interviews because he would like to talk with customers face to face about why they choose some loyalty cards and not others. However, he would also like to say something more generally about the use of loyalty cards by customers of SMEs in his local region. Samir decides to use the qualitative research interview as a way of facilitating the quantitative stage of his study. Working with a local SME, he first conducts interviews with six of their regular customers about their behaviours regarding loyalty cards more generally. From the data analysis, he analyses a range of factors that impact on loyalty card use. He then designs a questionnaire about the relative importance of those factors to send to 100 customers so that he can make some general statements about loyalty card behaviour. Hence, Samir is using interviews as part of a mixed methods research design.

The interview can also be used as part of a multi-method study where different data from different methods can provide different insights into a given organizational phenomenon. Interviews can be used alongside other qualitative methods such as diary studies or observation, for example. The latter is particularly the case with case study or ethnographic designs which rely on a range of different methods, as can be seen in Box 1.3.

1.3   Using interviews in a multiple qualitative methods design

The focus of Ravi's MBA dissertation is on evaluating the success of a leadership training programme in his own organization. Ravi knows that there are some complex issues when researching your own organization, particularly in relation to how people respond to you in your role as researcher rather than in your role as colleague. He believes that in using his own organization as a case study, the best way to seek a range of views about the leadership programme is to use different qualitative methods together. Case studies typically involve the use of a variety of methods. Ravi has already read and analysed some of the important company policy documents that relate to the leadership programme, such as the staff development strategy of the organization. Hence, next he plans to conduct five exploratory key stakeholder interviews with those involved in designing the programme and also ask 10 of those who have just completed the programme to keep a diary for three weeks afterwards to record instances in the workplace where they believe their experience on the leadership programme has impacted on the decisions that they make. Hence, Ravi is using the interview as part of a case study design using multiple qualitative methods.

INDIVIDUAL AND GROUP INTERVIEWS

The interview is not necessarily confined to individuals alone and one alternative is to conduct a group interview. There is a variety of different types of group interviews – for example, Delphi studies where the opinions of various experts are sought in turn, or focus groups which have become particularly popular in the market research field. Steyaert and Bouwen (2004) suggest that there are two key characteristics that differentiate between group methods. The first is whether the group is a naturally occurring group within an organization, for example a project group or work team, the alternative being a group manufactured for research purposes, for example a focus group. The authors suggest that this is not always a clear distinction and that the role of the researcher is important here in the extent to which they have an influence on creating the group context. The second characteristic is the aim of the researcher. Here, the researcher could be seeking the exploration or description of ideas within the group, where the aim is to understand the context. An alternative is where the researcher is seeking a generation of ideas, for example about a re-organization of systems in the workplace. A further aim of the research could be to actually intervene within a given group, for example a team-building intervention in an already existing group or the creation of a taskforce group to plan an intervention in job design. In each of these situations, a group interview can be used. As with any other form of interview, there should be a clear rationale for why the group interview is considered appropriate and how it fits with the research question and research design. A summary of the different types of group method within which interviews can be used can be found in Table 1.1.

Table 1.1 Different types of group method

Group setting/purpose of research	Natural	Created
Exploration	Work groups/group observations	Group interviews/focus groups
Generation	Work-team study/group experiments/role plays	Group simulations/group meetings
Intervention	Team building/action research	Project groups/taskforce analysis

Source: Steyaert and Bouwen (2004: 141).

APPROACH TAKEN WITHIN THIS BOOK

As has been stated, the interview offers the researcher a range of opportunities. In the chapters that follow, we consider what some of these opportunities are. An underlying assumption throughout is that the interview will be the basis of a graduate research project and that the reader may have had little or no previous experience of conducting a research interview. The chapters that follow address the relevant issues the prospective interviewer might encounter as they plan their research study. Chapter 2 introduces readers to the different types of interviews that can be conducted and introduces a framework that can be used to differentiate the different types of interviews in use, and inform the choice of one interview design over another. Chapter 3 introduces the different components of the research interview and provides advice about each of the stages of interview design from the design of questions to piloting. Chapter 4 considers the interview itself and focuses on some of the practicalities of conducting an interview, including interview location and transcription. It also considers a range of contextual issues the researcher needs to bear in mind that potentially complicate the process. These issues include ethics, power, reflection and reflexivity. Chapter 5 provides some more detailed illustrations of how interviews are used in the business, organization and management literature. Chapter 6 then reviews the advantages and disadvantages of using interviews and offers some suggestions about what makes a good interview. In the final sections, the next steps after the interview is complete, such as thinking ahead to data analysis, are considered.

My assumption in writing this book is that it will not be too onerous to read nor too long, therefore the expectation is that the reader will read it from beginning to end rather than dip in and out of the different chapters. The aim is that all of the key points are covered from the start to the finish of the interview process. The interview offers many opportunities for business, management and organizational researchers. One of the joys of qualitative research is the opportunity to access the interpretations and views of organizational participants. Conducting interviews can be an insightful, rich and interesting experience, but can also be frustrating and problematic at times. Reading this book cannot guarantee that you are more likely to experience the former, but the intention is that you feel better prepared in approaching interviews as part of your research endeavours.

2

UNDERSTANDING RESEARCH INTERVIEWS

INTRODUCTION

The aim of this chapter is to introduce readers to the different types of interviews that can be conducted in organizational and management research; to introduce a framework which can be used to differentiate the different types of interviews in use; and to highlight what influences the choice of one interview design over another. We start with a consideration of some of the different conceptualizations of the interview within the business and management literature and then consider the different types of interview a researcher can use.

HOW CAN WE UNDERSTAND INTERVIEW VARIATION?

Within the organizational literature, there are numerous typologies of research interviews. These focus on the dimensions or continua along which interviews differ. Here, we consider two ways of characterizing different types of interviews. The first relates to the epistemological commitments that underpin the interviewer's research. These are important in that they frame how a researcher interprets the researched and the research process more generally. The second concerns the level of structure in the interview, which is a key feature discussed in much of the literature on interviewing.

PHILOSOPHICAL APPROACH

An important factor that influences the nature of the research interview is the underlying philosophical assumptions of the researcher. For example, the standardized or more structured interview is likely to be informed by positivist epistemological commitments, where the emphasis is on generating objective data which represents some truth about the interviewee's world. As such, the intention will be to minimize any contamination that may occur as a result of the social or active nature of the interview, including the impact of the interviewer on the interviewee.

King (2004a) differentiates between three sets of ontological and epistemological assumptions underlying qualitative interviews: the realist, phenomenological and social constructionist. Definitions of ontology and epistemology can be found in Box 2.1.

2.1   Defining philosophical assumptions

Ontology is the philosophical study of being, existence and reality. Ontology deals with questions regarding whether or not entities can be said to exist. If we subscribe to a realist ontology, then we believe that the phenomena we are interviewing about – for example, job satisfaction, marketing strategy or financial markets – exist as real entities in the social world before we enter it. If we subscribe to a constructionist ontology, then we believe that the phenomena we investigate do not exist independently from ourselves as researchers. Rather, they are artificial creations that come into existence through our talk or discourse. The world does not exist independently of us.

Epistemology is the theory of knowledge and the criteria by which we can know what does, and does not, constitute warranted or scientific knowledge. Interviewers who take an objectivist approach to epistemology assume that the social sciences are similar to the natural sciences in that researchers seek to explain and predict by searching for regularities and causal relationships, avoiding contaminating the research setting. Interviewers who take a subjectivist approach to epistemology assume that the researcher does not have a privileged vantage point. Rather, we all interpret and make sense of the world in different ways and the interviewer can only report their own interpretations without any claim to privilege.

Within a realist approach, the interviewer is keen to access the interviewee's understanding of a particular organizational phenomenon that is seen to exist outside of the person and then compare their account with other interviewees. Within a phenomenological approach, the concern is with the researcher reflecting on how their own presuppositions may impact on the data collected, as well as exploring the life world of the interviewee. Within social constructionist approaches, the interview is seen as the co-production of a text, rather than as an account of any real-world phenomenon. Alvesson and Sköldberg (2000) highlight that from a constructionist position, how interviewees represent reality in the interview situation may have more to do with how they are understanding and constructing the discursive context of the interview itself, rather than being any reflection of an enduring, external reality. Therefore, the interview from this perspective is a very different encounter from how it is perceived by those working in other epistemological traditions such as positivism.

There are also other traditions where the underpinning philosophical commitments may involve seeking to empower participants. Limerick and O'Leary (2006: 108), for instance, in their discussion of how feminist qualitative research can inform the management field, reflect on their use of interviews in a study of women's careers as a way of giving women a 'voice' in the 'co-creation of knowledge claims'. Similarly, Mirchandani (2003) describes how open-ended qualitative interviews in the context of an anti-racist feminist theoretical approach enabled her to identify the use of emotion work by the interviewees, which was not the intention of the original research study.

A further way of considering different positions on interviews is to explore the different knowledge claims that are enabled by different stances. Inevitably, such distinctions will also be informed by an epistemological approach. Alvesson (2011) characterizes three major positions taken on interviewing: neo-positivism, romanticism and localism. Neo-positivism is similar to what King (2004a) identifies as a realist approach in that the intention is to access via the interview the truth about behaviour, attitudes, interests, and so on, in as objective a way as possible. In this way, the aim is that the knowledge generated can be generalized. In a romanticist approach, the interview is seen as an authentic dialogue fostered in good interpersonal relationships. The aim here is to achieve a deep understanding of the research issue through building trust with the interviewee so that both parties can jointly construct meaning and access organizational reality. Such an approach is associated with interpretivism in its broadest sense. Localists, on the other hand, are interested in the interview in itself as a contextually specific process. Therefore, an interview is a genre of conversation that should be studied as such, rather than a tool for data collection (Silverman, 2006; Alvesson and Ashcraft, 2012). Hence, localists see the interview as ontologically different from neo-positivists and romanticists. Here, the interview is not a reflection of some pre-existing reality but rather a distinctive social encounter.

How does the novice interviewer account for these different epistemological stances in their own approach to interviews? The first stage is to recognize our own epistemological assumptions and how they might influence how we frame the interview. The key point here is that the format and process of an interview will be influenced by the epistemological approach of the research overall, making this an important factor that influences the variety found in management and organizational research interviews (see Box 2.2).

2.2   Understanding your epistemological approach

Wen Wen is studying for a Masters degree in Accounting and is looking forward to the prospect of conducting some original research for her dissertation. She is interested in how auditors make evaluative decisions about company accounting practices and is privileged to have gained access to a regulatory body and to firms of auditors in her home country to conduct her research. The plan is to conduct interviews with a number of auditors to find out the intentions behind accounting standards. Although initially finding epistemology a daunting concept, Wen Wen is keen to be clear about her own philosophical stance. Her view is that there is a real world out there but that auditors experience and interpret some of the practices of companies in different ways within that real world. After reading around the subject, she decides that her approach to how she understands auditors' practice is informed by a realist ontology. However, because she believes that auditors will all interpret those practices differently, her approach to epistemology is interpretivist. Hence, her interviews will explore how these different interpretations impact on their practice.

INTERVIEW STRUCTURE

It is common to differentiate interviews according to the level of structure the interviewer uses to determine the progression of the interview according to their pre-existing ideas; the research questions; and the resulting questions in the interview schedule. Interviews are usually differentiated as structured, semi-structured or unstructured. Structured interviews will have a set script of questions that all interviewees will be asked in the same order, therefore ensuring consistency across interviews. In semi-structured interviews, there will be a list of questions and prompts but the interviewer deviates from the schedule, depending on the responses of the interviewee. Hence, there is the opportunity to follow up on interesting issues that the interviewee raises that may not have previously been considered by the interviewer. With unstructured interviews, although the research may have a theme or topic to focus the discussion on, there are few, if any, pre-formulated questions, so the interview can go in any direction as a result of the interviewer's or interviewee's interpretations of the topic. Clearly, the more unstructured the interview becomes, the more active thinking the interviewer has to do throughout the interview in relation to questioning. Therefore, a high level of skills is required in order to manage the interview which means the unstructured version may not be a suitable choice for a Masters dissertation.

The structure of an interview is linked to its purpose. Usually, the more structured formats are associated with the quantification of the data generated, whereas in qualitative approaches typically interviews are semi-structured, or unstructured, encouraging the interviewee to talk at length around a subject and shape the direction of the interview as necessary. Therefore, as King (2004a) suggests, one of the key things that differentiates the various approaches to interviews is the relationship between the interviewer and the interviewee. In highly structured interviews, the aim is to minimize any bias that may occur from the role of the interviewer, hence the standardization of the questions and format. Within more qualitative, less unstructured approaches however, it is recognized that the interviewee takes an active role in constructing the nature of the interview, and can direct it as appropriate.

The distinction between different levels of structure in questioning is not as straightforward as it initially seems. For example, there are a number of different ways of structuring qualitative interviews designed to generate open-ended data in a particular format, such as those that use repertory grid, cognitive mapping or critical incident. Hence, in terms of thinking further about the different types of interview structure available, we now focus on how we might characterize interviews based on their purpose. We now explore these differences in more detail. Table 2.1 summarizes the different types of interviews according to level of structure and purpose and therefore provides a summary of what follows.

Table 2.1 Purposes of interviews

Level of structure	Type of interview	Purpose of interview
Structured	Information gathering	Gather attitude/opinion data that can be quantified for analysis
	Hypothesis testing	Gather data for quantification and theory testing
Semi-structured, thematic format	Exploratory	Gather information about a given topic
	Theoretical	Generate data to enable theory development
Semi-structured, distinctive format	Event based	Generate data through understanding how interviewees make sense of different events
	Comparative	Generate data through forcing the interviewee to make comparisons
	Narrative	Encourage interviewees to tell stories from their own perspective
	Biographical	Gain insights into the interviewee's experiences through chronological reflection
	Visual techniques	Generate data by encouraging participants to project their own views or feelings onto a visual stimulus
Unstructured	Phenomenological	Gain insights into an individual's lifeworld

DIFFERENT TYPES OF INTERVIEW STRUCTURE FOR DIFFERENT PURPOSES

In this section, we consider the link between structure and purpose by examining different varieties of structured, semi-structured and unstructured interviews.

Structured interviews

As previously mentioned, the key purpose of structured interviews is usually to enable the objective comparison of interview data across interviewees, hence enabling the qualitative data collected to be quantified for analysis. Here, we can categorize them into two different types: information gathering and hypothesis testing.

Information gathering

In some research projects, the interviewer may be interested in collecting data regarding the attitudes or opinions of organizational members or the general public on a particular issue. However, they may choose to do this as part of an interview rather than as part of a questionnaire survey. Furthermore, they might be keen to be able to quantify the qualitative data so that it can be content analysed at a later stage. The aim may be to run some statistical tests on the data and make some conclusions regarding the generalization of the findings. Hence, the purpose of the structured interview in this case is information gathering, and a standardized interview schedule enables all interviewees to be asked the same questions in the same order. The structured nature of the interview also means that, in theory, it will be reliable in that the interviewee will produce the same answers regardless of the characteristics of the interviewer. In many cases, the structured interview is equivalent to a questionnaire that is administered by the researcher rather than self-administered (see Ekinci, 2015). For example, Cassell, Nadin, Gray and Clegg (2002) used a structured interview survey with 100 SME managers to ascertain their usage of a variety of human resource practices. In practice, structured interviews are more usually thought of as questionnaires completed by an interviewer rather than the interviewee (see Ekinci, 2015). An example of a structured interview for information gathering can be found in Box 2.3.

2.3   Designing a structured interview for information gathering

Hui is studying for a Masters degree in Management Strategy. As part of her research, she is interested in the extent to which SMEs are using a range of different tools for strategic analysis of the environment, for example stakeholder analysis and SWOT analysis. Hui is keen to conduct a structured interview where she gathers information about whether companies use these kinds of strategic tools and how effective they are. She is keen to talk with managing directors in person rather than asking them to fill in a questionnaire and has arranged a number of telephone interviews with local companies. Hui wants to be able to statistically analyse the data collected so that she can make generalizations about how effective different tools of analysis are. Within the interview schedule, Hui has a list of different tools such as balance scorecard, PEST analysis, SWOT analysis, and so on. The plan is that each managing director will be asked whether they use each of those tools and asked to answer yes or no. They will then be asked to rate how effective they think those tools have been on a scale of 1 to 5. Through using the structured interview to gather information in this way, Hui will be able to statistically analyse the managing directors' views of the success or otherwise of the different strategic tools.

Using an interview for hypothesis testing

When seeking to use an interview as a way to test theory, researchers are usually working within a positivist paradigm. In order to test hypotheses, it is important that the relevant variables are clearly operationalized to ensure the reliability and validity of measures. Hence, hypothesis testing can be problematic in interviews unless the interview is highly structured. Reliability is about the consistency of measures and validity focuses on whether a measure actually measures what it is supposed to measure. Replication is also seen as important, as is generalization. Therefore, in terms of reliability, a structured interview schedule means that each interviewee will be asked the same questions in the same order. The structured nature of the questions and ordering also mean that different interviewers should, in theory, generate the same response from interviewees, meaning that the interview as a research encounter is potentially replicable. The ability to generalize from interview findings depends on the sampling strategy and we will discuss this in more detail in the next chapter. It is difficult to meet these demanding criteria from an interview study, so if this is your aim, the more structure in the process the better! An example is offered in Box 2.4.

2.4 Designing a structured interview for hypothesis testing

Wayne is investigating gender differences in perceptions of organic products for his Marketing dissertation. He is interested in a range of products and is keen to access the views of enough customers so he can look at the impact of gender

(Continued)

(Continued)

differences. He is also interested in investigating the extent to which a positive attitude towards a product impacts on the customer buying the product for use. Wayne therefore wants to test three hypotheses in his research. Hypothesis 1 is that attitude towards a product is not related to intention to purchase the product. Hypothesis 2 is that there is no influence of gender on attitudes to green products. Hypothesis 3 is that there is no influence of gender on the intention to purchase green products. Given these hypotheses, Wayne has decided to have a structured interview where all interviewees are asked the same questions in the same order. The intention is that the data Wayne gathers can then be quantified for analysis so he can test his hypotheses. Wayne has decided to use a structured Likert scale to ask interviewees the extent to which they agree or disagree with a statement on a five-point scale. Wayne has structured his interview schedule into three sections. The first has statements about attitudes towards organic products including 'Using organic products is better for the environment' and 'Eating organic food enables children to have a healthier diet'. The second set of statements is related to the intention to purchase organic food – for example, 'I plan to buy some organic vegetables during the next week'. The final section of the interview has a range of demographic variables such as gender and age within it so that Wayne can test all three of his hypotheses.

SEMI-STRUCTURED INTERVIEWS: THEMATIC FORMAT

The area with the greatest variety and number of options is the semi-structured interview. There are some that have a pre-set format of questioning that the interviewer should follow whereas others are more open. To differentiate between these types, here I classify them as semi-structured interviews with a thematic format and semi-structured interviews with a distinctive format.

Included in this category are interviews where the interviewer has a particular topic or research question that they wish to investigate which they address by devising a list of thematic questions.

Exploratory semi-structured interviews

The purpose of this type of interview is to explore a particular organizational issue from a range of different perspectives. The interviewer devises a range of questions around particular themes that enables them to gather information about the topic or question. For example, I may be interested in exploring the views of international MBA students about their experiences of studying in the UK. Hence, I will devise a series of questions under different themes. These could include, for instance, their experiences of transitioning to live in the UK more generally; their experiences of the Business School culture; and their social life in whichever place they have chosen to live. These questions will be open-ended and will form the basis of my semi-structured thematic interview.

Theoretical semi-structured interviews

This interview is again semi-structured but here theory plays a role in how the interview questions are structured. In most cases, the data are collected to enable the development of theory. Therefore, the questions in the interview schedule may be thematically organized around exploring different theoretical aspects of an organizational phenomenon. For example, in researching how people experience decision making and fairness in organizations, I may be interested in drawing on theories of organizational justice. Therefore, I may thematically organize my interview schedule around the different types of organizational justice that have been identified in the theoretical literature on that topic, for example distributive, procedural and informational justice (see Colquitt et al., 2001). The intention is that the analysis of the data from the interview will enable me to develop theoretical insights into how organizational justice is experienced or perceived.

A further approach is where we want to use the interview data to develop theory using the processes of induction. Gill and Johnson (2010) suggest that induction involves moving from observation of the empirical world to an interpretation of those observations and theories about what has been observed. So, the researcher will develop theory through the process of analysing their interview findings. Here, the purpose of the interview is to generate data that can be analysed in such a way as to enable theory development (see Box 2.5).

2.5   Designing a semi-structured theoretical interview

Alfredo is interested in exploring how organizational commitment changes as a company goes through an organizational change project as part of his Masters programme in Human Resource Management. He is interested in exploring theories of organizational commitment in a qualitative way with employees. He is pleased to have gained access to a large local company that has just undergone a merger with a US-based multinational company. Alfredo wants to use the interviews to ask about the organizational commitment of interviewees both before and after the merger so he can explore theoretically how organizational commitment may

(Continued)

(Continued)

change over time. Alfredo has read some of the extensive literature on organizational commitment and knows that there are a number of different dimensions of commitment. Hence, his aim is to structure the interview into a series of themes that will address those different dimensions of organizational commitment so that his findings and analysis will enable him to comment theoretically on organizational commitment and change.

SEMI-STRUCTURED INTERVIEWS: DISTINCTIVE FORMAT

As noted earlier, there are a range of different formats that can form the structured part of the semi-structured interview. These usually form one part of the interview and then there is also space for other questions. Each of these can be used in an exploratory fashion or be used in the development of theory. The most often used ones are outlined in this section.

Event-based interviews

The aim of an event-based interview is to ask the interviewee to focus on a particular event and, in exploring their experiences of that event, to generate insights into how they explain various organizational phenomena. An event in this context could be a number of things – for example, an incident, a relationship, an experience or any other specific entity. One of the most popular event-based approaches is the critical incident technique (CIT) (Flanagan, 1954; Chell, 2004). Here, data are collected about a specific significant incident. Examples of the use of CIT in the literature include the study of entrepreneurship (Chell, 2004); service research (Gremler, 2004); and team performance (Druskat and Wheeler, 2003). In the interview, the interviewer asks the interviewee to describe a particular incident and then follows up with a series of questions about the incident. For example, if researching customer service or safety, the interviewer could say, 'Tell me about a time when you experienced good customer service' or 'Tell me about a time when you encountered a potential safety issue in your workplace'. After the initial identification of the incident, the interviewer goes through a series of follow-up questions. These could include questions such as what happened; when it happened; why it happened; the short- and long-term consequences of it happening; who was involved and why; how people responded; and how it was explained. At each stage, the interviewer can seek clarification and rich detail about the incident. Interviews may focus on more than one incident to look for patterns in an organizational phenomenon from the interviewee's perspective (see Box 2.6).

2.6   Designing a critical incident technique interview

Chelsea is studying for a Masters degree in Finance and Banking. Before start-ing her course, Chelsea had an internship with a large merchant bank. During her time with that institution, Chelsea became particularly interested in how mar-ket share announcements impacted on analyst behaviour. Having learnt about the efficient market hypothesis as part of her postgraduate programme, she is now keen to interview market analysts about their views regarding the impact of share announcements. Chelsea had read the relevant literature in the area and has decided that it would be useful to study the impact of share announcements by the top 10 companies in the FTSE index. She is in the lucky position that she has access to market analysts in the bank where she did her internship and they have agreed to be interviewed. Chelsea decides that she will use critical incident technique and she will ask interviewees to talk about their views of the impact of the share announcements of those 10 companies. Hence, each announcement will be treated as a critical incident. From hearing how interviewees talk about these specific incidents, she aims to generate insights into the extent to which markets are efficient.

Comparative interviews

The aim of these kinds of interviews is to encourage the interviewee to make distinc-tions based on comparisons. The most well-known of these techniques is the repertory grid. The repertory grid is based on George Kelly's personal construct theory (Kelly, 1955). Kelly believed that individuals were scientists who made sense of their worlds through drawing on their own set of personal constructs to make distinctions between phenomena. He created repertory grid technique as a way of accessing an individual's personal constructs. Originally devised for a therapeutic context, repertory grid is now used in a range of different management research areas and has been used to access – amongst other things – constructions of safety in the workplace (Gammack and Stephens, 1994); performance in manufacturing (Duberley et al., 2000); gender and performance (Shaw and Cassell, 2007); and organizational culture and change (Langan-Fox and Tan, 2011). The aim of the interview is to develop a detailed under-standing of the individual's different constructs and how they are organized. The process is that the interviewee is asked to make distinctions between a triad of ele-ments to create their own set of personal constructs.

The grid data can be analysed using either qualitative or quantitative techniques. A number of authors have pointed out that the grid in itself is not the only source of data to emerge from a repertory grid interview and that discussions whilst the grid is being produced are also informative. Gammack and Stephens (1994) describe the repertory grid as a 'conversational technology' to capture the nature of the talk that goes on in the interview as part of the process (see Box 2.7).

2.7   Designing a repertory grid interview

Mohammed is studying for a Masters degree in Marketing. For his dissertation project, he has chosen to do a piece of research that his supervisor is particularly interested in him investigating. The research question is what attracts students to apply to some business schools to study their Masters degrees rather than others. Mohammed has decided that the most appropriate way of accessing such insights is to use repertory grid technique. In seeking to elicit constructs, Mohammed will use a number of different business schools both in the UK and overseas for the elements. He will then interview students enrolled in Masters programmes at these different universities to see how their constructs highlight the different criteria they use when selecting a school to apply to.

Narrative interviews

The aim of the narrative interview is to encourage interviewees to tell stories about their own experiences of organizational phenomena. The choice of narrative interviews is informed by a constructionist stance in that the use of narratives or stories is seen as an important way in which individuals make sense of their organizational experiences. Therefore, the researcher can seek to access both individual and organizational narratives through their questioning. For example, individual narratives can focus on biographical elements such as career stories (Cohen and Mallon, 2001). Organizational narratives refer to stories about organizations which Czarniawska (1997) suggests are one of the main ways in which communication takes place in organizations. In seeking to access narratives and stories, we do not expect them to be true in a realist sense; rather, the expectation is that there will always be competing narratives for interviewees to draw on. Furthermore, the performative nature of the interview is particularly recognized here in that we know that when we ask people to tell stories, there is often an entertainment expectation involved (Gabriel and Griffiths, 2004).

Narrative interviews are used in a range of different areas of management and organizational research, though they are particularly found in research on change and identity. This reflects how many writers see narratives as a part of identity construction (e.g. Vaara, 2002) which has an important role in sensemaking (Weick, 1995). The recognition that narratives are temporal in that they change over time is why this approach is particularly popular amongst organizational change researchers. An example can be found in Box 2.8.

2.8   Designing a narrative interview

Sven is studying for a Masters degree in Operations and Supply Chain Management. He is interested in how the personal relationships between key individuals in different parts of a supply chain influence the success of that supply chain. In addressing this issue, he is keen to talk with the key organizational stakeholders in one supply chain about their relationships. In terms of accessing rich data about relationships, Sven decides to conduct a series of narrative interviews. The intention is to focus on the manager's stories of the stakeholders in the supply chain and how the relationships between them all have developed. His aim is to gain insights into the informal processes that underpin the effective operation of the supply chain, which often remain hidden.

Biographical interviews

The aim of the biographical interview is to gain insights into the interviewee's experiences through chronological reflection on their life more generally. An example of this approach is life history method. There is some overlap between this approach and individual narrative interviews in that if you ask someone to talk about their life you are asking them to tell their life story. Therefore, as Musson (2004) highlights, this approach focuses on prioritizing individual interpretations of their lives and events. As such, it is rooted within an interpretivist tradition where the concern is how individuals interpret and make sense of their organizational experiences. However, a whole range of research questions can be addressed by the biographical interview. Examples include the impact of gender, age or class on workplace experiences or socialization, career development or experiences of team working. A biographical interview is particularly useful when seeking to understand some of the complex processes that lead to different interpretations of the same organizational phenomena, as the assumption is that different life experiences help construct or inform different interpretations. One aspect that is distinctive to biographical interviews is that questions tend to be asked in a chronological order and the use of 'timelines' is an increasingly utilized way of doing this (e.g Mazzetti and Blenkinsopp, 2012). Box 2.9 provides an example of a biographical interview.

2.9   Designing a biographical interview

Julian is interested in conducting research for his MBA dissertation to further his own understanding of how leaders influence their followers. He knows that there is a lot of literature in this area, but his pre-MBA experience has taught him that

(Continued)

(Continued)

really successful leaders have a certain kind of charisma that it is often hard to identify and pin down. He suspects that there might be something interesting about successful leaders' early experiences of being led themselves which might contribute to the development of charisma. Julian is lucky that there is a network of senior leaders associated with the alumni organization of the school where he is conducting his MBA. So far, 10 of these leaders have agreed to be interviewed for Julian's research dissertation. Julian has decided that he will conduct biographical interviews with them all in that he will ask the leaders to talk through their careers and see if, through the analysis, he can ascertain the links between early career experiences of being led and a leader's charisma.

Visual techniques

There are a range of different techniques that are used as part of the interview to encourage participants to interpret visual stimuli. Visual images are a very powerful medium. For example, Stiles (2004) points out that long after the newspapers stopped talking about 9/11, the images of the aeroplanes hitting the twin towers remained in many people's memories. Given the impact of images, it is not surprising that visual techniques have long been used as part of an interview process. Projective techniques have had a long history in psychological research and emerged from therapeutic settings where the assumption derived from psychoanalytic theory was that an individual would project their own feelings onto a visual stimulus which could then be readily interpreted by the therapist. Examples of such techniques include the Thematic Apperception Test (Morgan and Murray, 1935) where respondents are invited to construct a story based on photographs and drawings, and the Rorschach *inkblot* test (Rorschach, 1942) where perceptions of inkblots are analysed. Such stimuli have the advantage of enabling the same stimulus to be shown to each interviewee.

More likely to be found in research interviews nowadays is the use of other types of visual methods. Here, photographs or pictures can be given to interviewees to interpret. Alternatively, interviewees can be asked to draw something, for example a person (Stiles, 2004), with the interviewer looking at patterns across the drawings of different interviewees. Drawings can also be used as part of focus group interviews as a way of stimulating discussion. Again, these methods are underpinned by interpretivist philosophical stances (see Vince and Warren, 2012). The use of visual images is helpful when you want to encourage people to talk about a subject that may not be that easy to talk about or when you are not sure where to start. It is also a useful way of encouraging creativity on behalf of the interviewee (see Box 2.10).

2.10 Using visual images in the interview

Lila is studying for a Masters degree in Corporate Communications. She is particularly interested in cultures of consumption and in how advertisers use images of celebrities from the popular media to appeal to young people and encourage them to buy their products. Lila thinks that there are particular sub-cultures of young people that might react negatively to some of the celebrities used in advertising campaigns and she is keen to explore whether this is the case or otherwise. Lila has a sample of undergraduate students who have agreed to be interviewed, each of whom feels happy with labelling themselves as a member of a particular sub-culture. As part of her interview schedule, Lila will show her interviewees examples of different advertisements and ask them a variety of questions about their responses to the visual data.

UNSTRUCTURED INTERVIEWS

More than any other approach, the unstructured interview is based on the recognition that it is the interviewee that guides the interview process rather than the interviewer. The questions are adapted according to the responses of the interviewee and will be different for different interviewees. Hence, these types of interviews are located within an interpretivist or constructionist stance and fit in with a romanticist view of the interview (Alvesson, 2011). There is no list of questions; rather, the interviewer focuses on building up rapport with the interviewee and encouraging them to open up and direct the talk in their own way.

Phenomenological interviews

One type of unstructured interview is the phenomenological interview. Cope (2005: 168) suggests that the aim of phenomenological inquiry is 'to understand the subjective nature of "lived experience" from the perspective of those who experience it, by exploring the meanings and explanations that individuals attribute to their experiences'. Therefore, the goal of the phenomenological interview is to gain a description or an insider account from an individual about a given phenomenon, such as entrepreneurship or management. There is little, if any, structure to the interview schedule and the interviewees are told of the overall topic of the research and are asked to tell their own story. The intention is that they will not be restricted by the imposition of the researcher's frame of reference or views which typically form the basis of the questioning in semi-structured interviews. The potential of such little control over the interview may be somewhat daunting for the graduate student and this is a risky approach for someone conducting their first piece of research. Although where in-depth accounts are sought phenomenological interviews have much to offer, the concern for a Masters student using this approach would be that if the data generated is not as rich as originally hoped for, there is little time available to recover the project overall.

SUMMARIZING INTERVIEW STRUCTURE AND PURPOSES

In summary, there are a variety of different ways of structuring interviews which all relate to the different purposes which an interview can serve. Therefore, when choosing the type of interview to use with a given research question, these are the issues to consider. The diversity in choices available for interview methods offers many interesting opportunities for the graduate researcher. We now turn to the question of how to prepare for the research interview.

 **3**

BASIC COMPONENTS OF RESEARCH INTERVIEWS

INTRODUCTION

The aim of this chapter is to outline what is required in preparing to conduct a research interview. The different components of the research interview will be introduced to provide advice about each of the stages of interview design. As such, the chapter addresses the following stages: choosing the interview format; designing the interview schedule; respondent selection; and piloting the interview. A key theme of the chapter is how to manage these different stages given the time constraints within which the research is conducted. We now address each of these stages in turn.

THE INTERVIEW FORMAT

Typically, people think of interviews as face to face or via the telephone, yet, increasingly, with the advancement of communication technologies, interviews can be mediated technologically. We now consider the different formats that the interview can take.

Interviewing face to face

Traditionally within the literature, the face-to-face interview has been viewed as the most appropriate given the opportunities for rich data collection that it provides.

Here, researchers draw attention to the subtle nuances that occur in face-to-face interaction. For example, Stephens (2007: 211) reflects on how when interviewing elites (in this case, macroeconomists) he realized that a qualitative face-to-face interview 'affords the interviewer the opportunity to continually re-mould the inter-action to their needs and interests through visual cues and small utterances'. Hence, it is the presence of visual cues that is seen as distinctive here. Visual cues extend beyond those which facilitate rapport through being able to see the interviewee. Additionally, a face-to-face interview offers the opportunity to observe and collect extra types of data, for example through observing the interviewee's environment. When conducting an interview as part of case study research, it may also be pos-sible to collect documents that the interviewee makes reference to, by asking if it is possible to take a copy away, for example. Despite these advantages however, where people have conducted research on the similarities and differences between face-to-face and telephone interviews (see Sturges and Hanrahan, 2004), they have suggested that the quality of data generated may be similar, although clearly the processes are different. Therefore, it is not necessarily the case that a face-to-face interview is always better.

Interviewing face to face via Skype

With the increasing use of the internet and familiarity with internet tools, one option for the interviewer is to conduct interviews through Skype. Skype offers a number of advantages. The interviewer and interviewee both still have access to visual cues and the researcher can easily record both the audio and visual interaction of the interview through simple software downloaded onto their work station (Hanna, 2012). However, sufficient forethought is required when planning a Skype interview to address some of the issues that emerge from the reliance on technology. It is important, for instance, to ensure that you have a back-up way of communicating with the interviewee should the technology fail, such as having a back-up phone number ready in advance. Furthermore, my experience suggests that it is advisable not to schedule back-to-back interviews in case you encoun-ter any problems with the connection or the technology more generally and you end up being behind schedule. It is also useful to keep other internet traffic to a minimum during the interview so that you do not compromise the bandwidth you need for Skype. As with other interview formats, it is important to check out which technology produces the best results before you start to interview and it may be that a headset with a built-in microphone enhances the quality of the interview.

The biggest advantage of Skype is that you can interview at a distance so it is particularly appropriate where interviewees are not easily accessible, for example in other international locations or time zones.

Telephone interviews

Another way of compensating for distance or time pressures is the telephone inter-view. Research which compares the outputs of different types of interviews highlights the importance of the nature of the pre-existing relationship between the interviewer and the interviewee, so if you have to interview by telephone the way in which you establish the relationship initially with the interviewee is key (Sturges and Hanrahan, 2004). For example, you may still be able to recruit participants face to face or engage in preparatory activities via email to establish a relationship before the telephone interview takes place.

There are some situations where a telephone interview is particularly appropriate. Apart from the consideration of distance, it may be more appropriate when discuss-ing sensitive topics or when respondents are more generally hard to reach. Sturges and Hanrahan (2004) also suggest that telephone interviews incur less cost and are appropriate when there are potential researcher safety issues. Holt (2010) further highlights a series of advantages that emerge from the lack of context that is asso-ciated with telephone interviews. She suggests that there is less intrusion into the interviewee's lives and that the researcher is less likely to make analytic leaps when they have less contextual information available. As she points out: 'there is no need to consider the use of telephones for narrative interviewing as a second-best "option": indeed, there may be sound ideological, methodological and practical reasons why it may be a more favourable mode than the often "default mode" of face-to-face inter-viewing' (Holt, 2010: 120).

Online interviews

A further option is to interview online. Morgan and Symon (2004) suggest that lit-tle has been written about how electronic interviews have been used so far in the organizational field, but that they offer considerable potential, such as the advantage of allowing busy people to take part in an interview when it suits them (e.g. James and Busher, 2006). However, they do raise a distinctive set of issues. Jowett, Peel and Shaw (2011: 358) suggest that one limitation of online interviewing that is often missing within the current literature is the amount of time it takes to produce the same amount of data that would be forthcoming from a face-to-face interview. In their study, the online interviews lasted about three hours yet produced about half the amount of data that an hour-long face-to-face interview would have produced. So, the initial time savings anticipated might not necessarily appear.

A key issue here is whether the interview is synchronous or asynchronous. If syn-chronous, then the interviewer will type in a question to which the interviewee will respond and so the interview continues taking place in real time. If asynchronous, the interviewer will pose a question and the interviewee will answer at a convenient point, hence there are breaks in the interview process. Morgan and Symon (2004) and

James and Busher (2006) both suggest that the potentially asynchronous nature of online interviewing means that both interviewee and interviewer have time to reflect on their responses, and indeed their questioning. This makes for a different process than occurs in the other types of interviews we have discussed so far. On the one hand, it may generate a rich form of reflection that cannot occur in real time interviewing due to the lack of time available. On the other hand, it means that the spontaneous nature of responses is removed.

One key advantage of conducting an interview online is that there is no need to record and transcribe the interview once it has been conducted in that all the answers are there in the thread. Hence, this saves a considerable amount of effort and cost for the researcher. A disadvantage is that the interviewer loses control over the interview scheduling process more generally as the interviewee chooses to respond when they want to.

Choosing a format

A number of considerations should influence which format the interviewer chooses to use. Accessibility of the interviewees is important as is the technology available. The nature of the research and the research question are also pertinent in relation to what interviewees may be happy to discuss in different formats. The most important thing is that the interviewer has a clear rationale for the choice of format. A final important consideration here is that of timing and the pressures within which postgraduate students are often working in order to complete their dissertation. Organizing face-to-face interviews with busy people is often difficult and other forms of interviewing such as telephone and online may be seen as less intrusive for the busy interviewee and therefore easier to schedule.

DESIGNING THE INTERVIEW SCHEDULE

The questions to be asked form the basis of what is known as the interview schedule. After a sufficient preamble, the questions are listed in order on the schedule so that the interviewer can pursue them appropriately with the interviewee through the interview. Asking the appropriate questions is at the nub of the interview process and the success of the research project overall can depend on asking the right questions. We now consider the different types of questions to consider when planning the interview schedule.

Interview preamble

The first part of the interview schedule is the preamble. The intention of this stage is to provide the interviewee with information about the research. This information can cover a number of different areas – for example, details of the interviewer; the purpose of the research; who is funding the research; a summary of the questions to be asked; why the interviewee has been chosen to take part; assurances regarding confidentiality; and some comment about how the research will be used (see Box 3.1).

3.1   Example of an interview preamble

Below is an example of an interview preamble. This comes from an interview study that Vicky Bishop and I conducted with taxi drivers about their experiences of customer abuse at work:

My name is Cathy Cassell and I am part of a research team at Manchester University who are exploring how taxi drivers deal with difficult customers. I will ask you some in-depth questions about your perceptions and experience of this. I will also ask you to tell me some stories about what life as a taxi driver is like.

There are no right or wrong answers. We are just interested in your experiences of taxi driving. We will not use your name in any of the write-ups of the research and we will make sure that quotes used cannot be identified with you. I would like to record this interview in order to transcribe it later. Nobody else besides me and my research team at Manchester will listen to these recordings or read the transcripts. Is this OK?

Questioning

In structuring the interview schedule, a range of different types of questions can be used. Some of the different types of questions available to the interviewer are outlined below.

Open versus closed questions

The use of open or closed questions depends on the overall structure of the interviews. For example, if we are conducting a structured interview where the intention is hypothesis testing, then we would want to use as many closed questions as possible. In a semi-structured interview, we would assume that most of the questions would be open questions where you are encouraging the interviewee to talk rather than closing off their range of potential answers. For example, an open question would be 'Tell me about how you became a university professor'. This question would encourage the interviewee to start at whatever place they felt appropriate to talk about their path to that job position. An example of a closed question would be 'What is your job title?' This is a closed question because the interviewee can only offer a short specific answer to it, rather than being encouraged to elaborate. Other closed questions are those that invite the interviewee to answer either 'yes' or 'no', for example 'Have you ever experienced bullying at work?' Both open and closed questions can be used in the same interview. As well as open or closed questions, there are different types of questions that are appropriate for different stages of the interview.

Opening questions

The first few questions in the interview are crucial for both setting the agenda and making the interviewee feel comfortable. Hence, it is useful to ask some general and relatively uncontroversial questions at this early stage. For example, some potential first questions are: 'Can you tell me a bit about yourself and your job?', 'How did you come to work here?', 'What do you like about your job?', 'What do you dislike?' Each of these questions is designed to encourage the interviewee to talk about something they would feel comfortable about discussing and where they would have quite a lot to say. Therefore, the aim of the opening questions is to ease the interviewee into the interview.

Other questions

The questions that follow in the interview schedule should be organized to address the research question and fit with the purpose of the interview. So, these will be different for a narrative than an event-based interview, for example. If conducting a critical incident technique interview, then the questions will focus on a series of incidents. Despite these differences, it is important that questions are divided into meaningful sections. These could be around various themes or different aspects of the research question.

Prompt questions

The aim of a prompt question is to encourage an interviewee to further expand on their answer. Prompt questions can be both planned and unplanned. It is worth anticipating a number of prompt questions by including them in the interview schedule. In a series of interviews I conducted with Vicky Bishop about taxi drivers' experiences of customer abuse, one of the questions in the interview schedule was: 'Do you talk about abuse with others after the event?' Here, there were three follow-up prompts to encourage drivers to expand on their answer: other drivers, friends, and family. If the driver has not mentioned any of these groups in their response to the question, then these would be used to gather more detail about how incidents of abuse are managed and dealt with. The interviewer can also come up with some unplanned prompts as required.

Other ways of using prompt questions, apart from seeking to gain more detail, can be through the use of interpretive questions such as 'If I understand you correctly...' Here, the interviewer is encouraging the interviewee to expand through their request for clarification. Another way of prompting more response is to suggest an oppositional statement to seek a view, for example 'an alternative view would be...'.

Finishing questions

The interview should conclude in such a way where the interviewee feels comfortable that they have had their say and the interviewer feels satisfied that all their areas of interest have been covered. In achieving this goal, it is important to think carefully about the questions at the end of the schedule. The interview should ideally finish on a positive note so any controversial or more sensitive questions should be left to the middle of the schedule. As a final question, the interviewee is usually asked if there is anything else they would like to say or add to what they have already said. The interviewer should also explain what will happen next in terms of feeding back any findings from the research. You might also want to take the opportunity to ask the interviewee if they know anyone else who might like to be interviewed, particularly if you are using a snowball sampling strategy. Finally, you should of course thank the interviewee for their time and explain how their contribution is important.

Demographic questions

As part of the interview, it is likely that the interviewer will want some basic demographic details from the interviewee such as ethnicity, age, job title or whatever has particular resonance for the research question. Here, the interviewer does not necessarily need to ask these directly of the participant; rather, they can be given a checklist of categories to tick. Box 3.2 provides an example of a checklist of demographic questions.

3.2 Example of an interview demographic variables checklist

Imagine that you were interviewing SME owners about a particular subject relating to their business. Below is a checklist of potential demographic variables that could be important:

(Continued)

(Continued)

Variable	Answer (to be filled in by interviewer)
Interview reference number	
Name	
Date and time of interview	
Interview type (initial/follow-up)	
Interview location	
Gender	
Self-defined ethnicity	
Name of the business	
Nature of the business	
Number of employees	
Length of time in that business	
Location of the business	
Any additional information	

There is some debate about where these should come in the interview schedule. My own preference is to put them at the end, whilst other researchers prefer to put them at the beginning. Wherever they are placed, it is important that you only seek demographic data that is relevant to the research question, rather than seeking out unnecessary information you might not need or use. For example, if studying work-life balance, then the number of children an interviewee has might be important to know, but it may be irrelevant to other research questions. If you are seeking to classify people on various demographic variables, it is also important that you use appropriate categorical terms, such as definitions of different ethnic groups.

RESPONDENT SELECTION: CHOOSING WHO TO INTERVIEW

A key issue in the conduct of any piece of research is who is to take part. Talking to the right people is fundamental to being able to answer the research question, but who the right people are is not necessarily a straightforward question. We now consider some of the different approaches that are taken to respondent selection in interview research.

Probability and non-probability sampling

A key distinction in sampling more generally is the issue of probability. Probability sampling, which is used mainly in quantitative research, is based on the assumption that you know the chance or probability of each person being selected as part of the sample, that is, each individual has an equal chance of being selected. Qualitative research relies on non-probability sampling and sample sizes will be smaller than with quantitative work. Types of non-probability sampling include purposive, theoretical, opportunistic and convenience, and snowball.

In terms of sampling, the first decision is usually about the population or 'the whole set of entities that decisions relate to' (Easterby-Smith et al., 2008: 212). Examples of populations include all women, female entrepreneurs, female entrepreneurs in South Yorkshire, etc. It is important that you can clearly specify the boundaries of the population from which the sample is drawn. The sample is the sub-set of population who you will interview. If your interview study is structured and informed by a positivist approach and you are keen to test hypotheses, then you will need to ensure that your sample is representative and therefore you will need a form of probability sampling (Easterby-Smith et al., 2008). The first thing to do is to create a sampling frame where every single element to be included in the sample can be identified. From there, you can decide which method of sampling to progress. Methods include simple random sampling where all sub-sets of the frame have an equal chance of being selected and systematic sampling where, rather than selecting interviewees randomly, a particular criterion is applied, for example every tenth person on a list. Other sampling methods are based on the opportunities to sample from important sub-groups. Examples include stratified sampling where sampling is done equally within different groups or 'strata' and quota sampling where the population is first divided into mutually exclusive sub-groups and then sampling is conducted within those groups. If your interviews are more semi-structured and qualitative, then it is likely that you will use non-probability sampling. The different types of non-probability sampling are detailed below.

Purposive sampling

Here, members of a sample are chosen with a 'purpose' to illustrate or represent a particular type in relation to a key criterion. Ritchie and Lewis (2003) suggest that there are two aims with this form of sampling – first, to ensure that all key constituencies of relevance are covered; and second, to ensure that within each of the key criteria some diversity is included. If our study is of the experiences that female entrepreneurs in South Yorkshire have of setting up their own business, in terms of constituencies of relevance we may want to make sure that the sample covers those who are single business owners, those in family businesses and those in partnerships. In relation to diversity, we may want to include women of different ages, of different ethnic backgrounds and some who have children and some who do not.

Theoretical sampling

Theoretical sampling is associated with the development of grounded theory (Glaser and Strauss, 1967). It involves choosing new participants to interview who can be compared with those who have already been studied. This suggests that the interviewer does not necessarily have a clear indication of who will comprise the total sample when the interviews start. The choice of who to interview next depends on what is most likely to enable theory development. In the example of the study of the female entrepreneurs, it may be that after conducting say five interviews, we start to think that something that has a big impact on the success of business start-ups is the ethnic background of the interviewees. Therefore, in terms of theoretical sampling we may then choose to interview women from a wider range of ethnic backgrounds to develop this theoretical hunch.

Opportunistic sampling

With opportunistic sampling, the researcher takes advantage of unexpected or unforeseen opportunities in developing a sample, for example access to a given case study organization. Hence, the choice of who to interview will be determined by who is part of that organization. In relation to our example of studying female entrepreneurs, it may be that one meets a female entrepreneur whilst travelling or at a network event or in another context and the researcher seizes the opportunity to ask for an interview then.

Convenience sampling

Convenience sampling simply means that interviewees are chosen for ease of access, which might mean individuals who are already known to the student or the university or who have been passed on through other contacts. Accessing a sample that is opportunistic or convenient is fairly common within graduate-level research dissertations, as time constraints and other demands mean that it is often difficult to access those people a student might necessarily want to. However, it is still important that the convenience sample meets the demands of the research and enables the research questions to be answered. This needs to be stated explicitly within the dissertation.

Snowball sampling

A snowball sampling strategy is where the sample grows because one informant then recommends another informant to the interviewer. Hence, the metaphor of the snowball is used. In the same way as the snowball grows as it is rolled through the snow, so the sample grows in a similar way. In the example of interviewing female entre-preneurs, we may ask one interviewee if she can possibly recommend others who might be interested in being interviewed. A recommendation eases access to poten-tial future interviewees.

How many is enough?

One of the biggest concerns shared by those using qualitative interviews when conduct-ing dissertation research is what sample size is considered large enough to be credible (Saunders, 2012). Whereas there are clear guidelines for appropriate numbers when conducting quantitative research, where certain numbers are required to enable statis-tical claims to be made, there are no such guidelines in qualitative research. There are, however, a variety of issues that help the consideration of sample sizes in qualitative research. One is the idea of saturation, however within the literature there is no agreed view on when saturation is achieved. One view is that you know it is time to stop inter-viewing when you stop hearing anything that is particularly new, therefore a form of empirical saturation has been achieved. A second is related to the claims that you want to make about your findings. It is difficult to make claims about groups that are not rep-resented in your sample, therefore you need to make sure that the key constituencies are adequately covered. Third is the role of interviews in the dissertation and the extent to which they are used alongside other types of data. If an interview study is part of a mixed methods design, then only a few interviews may be required and used in either an exploratory or confirmatory way. Fourth is the advice of your supervisor who will be familiar with the demands required of the dissertation and what is considered locally as an acceptable sample size. Of course, we should not forget that the quality of the sample is perhaps the most important issue in that it is crucial to select interviewees who can directly address your research questions and provide informative responses to what you need to know. Fewer interviewees with direct relevance to your research ques-tion may be better than many who have little knowledge of or interest in it.

PILOTING THE INTERVIEW

The interview schedule should always be piloted. This means that it should be prac-tised beforehand. Even though we may have had advice from a range of different people about the questions within it, we never know how interviewees will respond to the questions until we actually try out the schedule for real. Some interview schedules will need piloting more than once. For example, if using a repertory grid it is crucial that respondents understand the different elements you have selected to structure the grid. Hence, piloting is an important part of the process.

In seeking someone to pilot the interview with, it is useful if they are a member of the target population on which the sample is based. If your sample contains hard-to-access people and you do not want to lose one of them to the piloting process, then the second best option is to try to find someone with similar characteristics. When conducting a pilot interview, it is done as if it is the real thing, however it is important to ask the pilot interviewee what they think about the schedule and the interview overall. You could leave this to the end or ask them to interject with comments as you go through if they prefer. This could cover issues such as any questions they found difficult or uncomfortable; whether they thought any of it was repetitive; commentary about the length of the interview; and any other issues. It is useful to make a record of their comments and important to make changes to the interview schedule if appropriate as a result of their feedback. The record of comments can be referred to in the methodology section of the dissertation where, in the section on piloting, you can discuss how the interview changed – and improved – as a result of the pilot stage.

PREPARED TO GO!

Once the interview schedule has been piloted and adapted accordingly, then the researcher is fully prepared. In the next chapter, we turn to the process of conducting the interview.

4

CONDUCTING RESEARCH INTERVIEWS

INTRODUCTION

The aim of this chapter is to outline the conduct of the interview itself. As such, the chapter focuses on some preliminary practicalities such as arranging the interview and recording the data; the interview itself, including a consideration of the development of rapport; and what happens post-interview, for example after the recording device has been turned off. We then turn to some important considerations beyond those practicalities that emerge from the active nature of the interview, such as identity work, reflexivity, power, predictability and ethical practice.

PRELIMINARY PRACTICALITIES

There are a number of practicalities that need attention before the interview can take place. These include preparing the interviewee and selecting the interview location. These may seem like trivial issues but preparing for the interview appropriately can prevent potential difficulties being encountered at a later stage.

Preparing the interviewee

It is important that the interviewee knows what to expect from the interview. One way of doing this is to provide an interview information sheet that provides the relevant details. These can include the title of the project; who is involved with the research; who is funding it; and how the findings will be used. The aim is that any initial questions or concerns the interviewee may have about taking part in the research will be addressed. These details may be different depending on the target group of interviewees and the potential questions they may have. For instance, in the example provided in Box 4.1 from the study Vicky Bishop and I conducted with taxi drivers, our contacts in the industry suggested that one of the most important things we needed to organize in order to recruit drivers to the project was a parking space so that they had somewhere safe to park their cabs whilst being interviewed. Hence, this was highlighted in the interview information sheet. An example of an interview information sheet can be found in Box 4.1.

4.1   An interview information sheet

Below is an excerpt from a flyer which aimed to recruit taxi drivers for an interview study. This contains information about the project more generally, plus it seeks to answer any potential questions the interviewees may have.

Invitation to take part in a Manchester Business School research project

What is the project about?

We are conducting research about taxi drivers' experiences of customer behaviour. We are interested in your stories about customers and customer service and how this affects your working life. We will use the findings to feed into academic and policy debates about customer service in the workplace.

Who are we?

Professor Cathy Cassell and Dr Vicky Bishop from Manchester Business School (MBS). We are members of the University's *Fairness at Work Research Group* and we have previously conducted similar research with bus drivers and others.

What will my participation involve?

We will need to interview you about your experiences for a maximum of an hour. We can interview you in your cab in the MBS West Car Park on Booth Street West off Oxford Road. The interview will be recorded but all your comments will be kept confidential in any write-ups of project findings.

What will I get out of it?

The chance to have a tea break (coffee and biscuits provided); tell your stories; and contribute to the research of the University of Manchester. We will also give you a

£20 Love2shop voucher that can be used in most major high street stores such as Argos, Debenhams, Matalan and HMV.

How do I arrange an interview?

We will be interviewing on the following dates:

Monday 27 June, Wednesday 29 June, Thursday 30 June, Friday 1 July

Simply phone Sammy on 0161 ... to let us know you are free. We need about 10 minutes' notice to arrange for an interviewer to meet you outside MBS West Reception on Booth Street West, off Oxford Road. The interviewer will get you a drink and show you where to park.

For more information, contact:

Cathy: ***** or Vicky: *****

In some cases, interviewers may send the interview schedule or a summary of the interview questions to an interviewee beforehand so that they have the chance to reflect on them before the interview takes place. Given that there are different options here, it is important that you carefully consider the information that you will give to the interviewee and let them know what you expect them to do with it before the interview takes place.

Seeking consent

It is important that the interviewee gives their informed consent to take part in the interview before the interview commences. This is part of standard ethical practice (Holt, 2012) which we discuss more in the next chapter. Box 4.2 shows the typical questions that form the basis of an informed consent form.

4.2 Example questions from an ethics consent form

1. I confirm that I have read and understand the information sheet for the above study. I have had the opportunity to consider the information, ask questions and have had these answered satisfactorily.

(Continued)

(Continued)

2. I understand that my participation is voluntary and that I am free to withdraw at any time, without giving any reason.
3. I understand that any information given by me may be used in future reports, articles or presentations by the research team.
4. I understand that my name will not appear in any reports, articles or presentations.
5. I give my informed consent to take part in the above study.

_____	_____	_____
Name of Participant	Date	Signature
_____	_____	_____
Name of Researcher	Date	Signature

As can be seen in Box 4.2, these questions usually ask the respondent to agree that they have received sufficient information about the study; that they are happy to take part; and that they appreciate that their participation is voluntary and that they can leave at any time. The participant is asked to sign to indicate agreement to the interview. Within the consent form, there are also usually some guarantees about confidentiality and anonymity. It is also useful to specify that the researcher can use the participant's comments in write-ups of the research. This is important not only for your dissertation, but also in case you seek to publish from the research at some future date. The consent form can be sent to the participant beforehand, or can be handed to them in the interview, as long as it is signed before the interview commences. Other concerns regarding ethical practice are addressed later in this chapter.

Incentivizing interview participation

This is a tricky issue and there is some debate about the appropriateness of providing incentives for interview participation (Head, 2009). Patton (2002: 414) suggests that researchers need to be careful about incentives and not assume that they are necessarily needed or effective. The characteristics of the interview sample are an important consideration here. In some cases – for example, when interviewing professional employees – it may be that the interview is viewed as part of their daily job so payment would not be expected. This is different for lower-income groups however, where it is important to ensure that interviewees are not disadvantaged by taking part in a research study. In the taxi driver study, for example, we offered the drivers that took part a £20 shopping voucher. This was to acknowledge that in giving up their time to be interviewed they would be forsaking the opportunity of an hour's work. In previous work with manufacturing workers who were paid piecework (Duberley et al., 2000), I was part of a research team that negotiated that interviewees would be paid for their time according to the rate usually given for time spent in training. A further issue here is the need to be sensitive to how incentives may be perceived. Although the opportunity to enter into a draw to win an iPod may be attractive to a student population, it may be perceived as patronising by a senior management team. Overall, there is no clear consensus within the literature about incentivizing interview participation but the issue needs to be treated in a sensitive manner. It is particularly important to note that different universities may have different guidelines about incentives which will be embedded in their ethical codes. Therefore, before considering incentivizing research participants, you must consider your university's stance on this issue.

Arranging the interview

Arranging the interview can be a tricky process as often those whom the researcher wishes to interview as part of a business and management research project are busy people with full diaries. It is important to specify clearly the time demands of the interview. If you think you will need an hour, then an hour of the interviewee's time should be requested, rather than asking for half an hour and hoping they will have extra time available afterwards. Furthermore, it is useful to make sure that both parties have contact details in case there are any unforeseen hitches with scheduling. It is worth mentioning here that conducting interviews can be quite a tiring and emotionally draining process. My own experience is that three interviews a day with breaks in between is more than enough. If someone in an organization is scheduling the interviews for you, it is important to draw this to their attention.

Interview location

A further practical issue to challenge organizational researchers is the location of the interview (Cassell, 2008). The interview requires a relatively quiet and calm location. First, this is important if you are seeking to audio-record the interview. In theory, it might be pleasant to interview someone in a coffee shop, but recording devices will pick up the sounds of bubbling coffee machines and chatter in the background, thereby making the interview recording quite difficult to transcribe. Second, if the interview covers what may be viewed as confidential or sensitive material, then it is important to have a location that is relatively private. Furthermore, the choice of interview location is not neutral. Indeed, Herzog (2005: 25) argues that 'the choice of interview location (who chooses and what place is chosen) is not just a technical matter of convenience and comfort'. Rather, it should be analysed as part of the overall social context of the study, and be considered as having a role in both the interaction between the interviewer and the interviewee and the knowledge produced.

Locations can have significant meaning for the interviewee. In interviewing taxi drivers in the back of their taxi, on several occasions they would refer to the cab as their working world, with one driver saying 'Welcome to my abode' as they invited me in (Cassell and Bishop, 2014). Interviews I conducted jointly with Bill Lee about trade union learning initiatives often took place in trade union learning centres and as part of those interviews the interviewees would describe their surroundings and how they had acquired the computers, or there would be photographs of learners on notice boards, all of which enhanced our understanding of the issues that we were asking questions about. Interesting and important contextual data can be gained from interviewing in the respondent's working environment. Another example of the importance of location comes from the work of Johnson, Bristow, McClure and Schneider (2011). Their interest was in the job satisfaction of long-distance truck drivers. The interviews for their study took place at a large truck-stop next to an interstate highway. Drivers were interviewed for 10–15 minutes when they stopped to refuel their trucks. The authors outline how interviews took place at different times of the day and different times of the week over a period of three weeks and from that they secured a sample of 104 drivers for interview. This is a good example of how researchers, in seeking to access appropriate interviewees, need to go to the locations where they can be found.

A more difficult issue is associated with being invited into an interviewee's home to conduct the interview. Clearly, the convenience of this may make the opportunity likely, for example if the interviewee has childcare responsibilities or no opportunity to talk during work time. Also, some respondents may feel more comfortable being interviewed at home. However, the issue of researcher safety is important here in that the researcher may be vulnerable outside of a public environment, therefore some caution is required. For example, mechanisms should be in place so that somebody, perhaps the research supervisor or a friend, knows exactly where the researcher is going to interview. Also, a phone-in system, where the researcher phones in to that designated person after each interview to let them know that the interview has finished, is important.

Recording the interview

It is important that the researcher has some record of the interview. This can be in note form, in a digital audio recording, in a video recording or indeed through a combination of all three. For example, when making an audio recording of an interview it is useful to be able to make notes at the same time, so that any follow-up questions that come to mind can be noted. There are three key issues that impact on the decision of what medium to use to record the interview. The first relates to the kind of data required and how it will be analysed. For example, if the researcher plans to use some form of linguistic analysis of the data, such as discourse or conversation analysis, then it is important that a high quality recording is achieved. However, there is no need to video-record an interview unless the visual data are going to be used. Therefore, a clear rationale is required before the interview about why one particular recording format has been chosen over another. The second issue is the impact that the mode of recording will have on the interviewee and the interview process itself. Hayes and Mattimoe (2004) raise some of the issues associated with the audio recording of interviews in their discussion of the use of interviews in accounting research. These include the impact of the presence of the machine on the interviewee and the mundane processes associated with transcription. Interviewees may initially feel intimidated by the presence of the recorder, though in practice this concern often disappears once the interview is in full flow. Third, and most importantly, the interviewee must give their permission to be recorded before the interview starts. So, if this permission has not been established before the interviewer and interviewee meet for the interview, then the interviewer needs to have an alternative mechanism of recording available to them. A final point is that if the interview is to be audio-recorded it is important to invest in a good digital recorder. Although most mobile phones will now offer this option, the quality of recording gained is often not sufficient for the process of transcription that will necessarily follow.

THE INTERVIEW ITSELF

Now that the preparation has been done, we turn to the interview itself. A variety of considerations are addressed in the sections that follow where we go through the interview process in chronological order.

Starting the interview

In the previous chapter, the importance of choosing appropriate questions to start the interview was highlighted. At the start of the interview, the aim is to enable the interviewee to feel at ease so that they are ready to answer your questions in as full a way as possible. This is the key time to seek to manage rapport and develop a positive relationship. The importance of developing rapport is highlighted throughout the literature on qualitative interviewing and is seen as having a significant impact on the quality of the data collected. King and Horrocks (2010: 48) point out that the development of rapport does not necessarily mean that you ingratiate yourself with the respondent but rather it is about trust. They highlight how even though the respondent may have received written information about the research project this may have been misread or misinterpreted, so an important part of developing rapport is saying something regarding what the research is about and checking if the respondent has any questions. An interviewee who is not used to a research situation may feel quite nervous at this stage and be worried that they might not give the 'right answers' or deliver on what is expected, so it is also useful to reassure the interviewee at the start that you are interested in their responses, regardless of what they are. The interviewer may also be nervous, of course, so it is important to ensure that you are feeling secure about the questions you are going to ask; and that the technology – if used – is in good working order. Being certain about these technical issues enables you to devote more attention to the interviewee. As King and Horrocks (2010: 49) suggest, self-presentation is also important in creating a relationship. Interviewees will be making interpretations based on all aspects of your background and behaviour and the interviewer will usually be performing some kind of identity work (see Cassell, 2005), which we explore in more detail later. Hence, this will also impact on the development of rapport.

Managing timing and sticking to schedule

This is an important part of the interview process, given that the time scheduled for the interview may be limited. As a result of the piloting stage, the interviewer should have a rough idea of how long the interview will take and it is important that the schedule designed fits the proposed time slot. However, the main issue that is the most surprising for first-time interviewers is that interviewees do not necessarily stick to the script or the questions you ask them. Rather, they can digress into areas that may be of great interest to you, but also into others that are potentially of very little interest. A common dilemma the researcher faces is where interviewees either talk too much or too little. King (2004a) suggests that when faced with an over-communicative interviewee, the interviewer can seek to get them back on schedule in subtle ways, for example by saying 'Can we return to what you said earlier about ... as I found that very interesting'. In interviews I have conducted, I have also sought to intervene politely by saying something like 'I know you are a busy person and your time is precious so perhaps we could now talk about...'. The key thing is to seek to intervene in a tactful and respectful manner.

Perhaps of more concern is the interviewee who says little and seems hesitant to share their views. Here, there are a number of ways in which we can encourage people to talk further. It may be that there are good reasons for their hesitancy, for example if the topic is a particularly sensitive one. Here, perhaps the interviewer can offer reassurance and remind them that all answers will be treated in confidence. King (2004a: 18) suggests that if you are succeeding in framing questions in a very open manner, and still getting brief, shallow answers, a useful tool to use is silence. Instead of moving onto your next question, when the interviewee provides another terse response, pause for a few seconds. Very often, this will serve as a cue to the interviewee that you would like to hear more on the subject, and is less likely to annoy them than repeated probes of the 'Tell me more' type.

Sometimes, however, the interviewer can discern that the interviewee simply does not want to discuss something. This can then be clarified by the interviewer suggesting something like 'You seem a bit hesitant about this topic; would you prefer to move on?' This is preferable to encouraging the interviewee to disclose something that they would prefer not to. Furthermore, if the interviewee seems to be distressed, then the interviewer should offer them the chance to pause the interview for a short while and turn off the recording device.

Dealing with an unpleasant interviewee

Increasingly within the literature there is recognition that sometimes interview situations can be uncomfortable for the interviewer in that the interviewee may express opinions that are offensive to the interviewer. What does the interviewer do in this situation?

Sara Nadin (Nadin and Cassell, 2006: 213–14) recounts an interview situation where, as she tells it, 'I experienced an intense dislike for the employer being interviewed. I found his treatment of me patronising, and some of the views he expressed racist and sexist'. Sara noted this in the following way in her research diary: 'Aaaaggghhh!! … Arrogant pig. Who'd work for him???!!! Sexist bigot. Felt really uncomfortable … like a little girl who was being told how it was in the world of the small business MAN!!! Liked the sound of his own voice.' This initial reaction 'was further reinforced when transcribing the interview, vividly bringing back the whole experience, eliciting similar feelings of anger and irritation'. Sara highlights:

> the incident led me to reflect on the power dynamics of the interview situation and my role within that. This initially led me to question why I did not challenge his views and the implicit collusion signalled by remaining both silent and passive. This itself prompted consideration of whether indeed I should have challenged his views (did I have a right to do that?), and what I would do if it happened again.

Such a situation creates a dilemma for the interviewer. We want to gather data from the interviewee and there is no reason why we should expect them to share our views of the world. However, if we are in a situation where we feel threatened then we should terminate the interview as soon as possible. There is an increasing consideration within the literature of what happens when interviews go wrong, whether it is as a result of discomfort or other reasons such as the lack of data generated. A further interesting account is provided by Nairn, Munro and Smith (2005) who outline the anatomy of a 'failed interview', as a form of 'uncomfortable reflexivity'

(Pillow, 2003: 188). They suggest that in reflecting on why the research team originally classified the interview as a failure in data collection terms, they learned a considerable amount about the 'tenuous' nature of knowledge production which informed the later design of their study.

Finishing

As stated in the previous chapter, it is important that the final questions in the interview schedule ideally finish on a positive note. The development of rapport that has been accomplished through the interview process comes with some responsibilities on the researcher's behalf. Given the development of the relationship and the disclosure of the interviewee, the interview needs to finish appropriately. An interesting phenomenon that many interviewers experience relates to what happens when the recording stops. At this stage, the interviewee may visibly relax and share further information that has not previously been captured, almost as if they are now free to talk 'off the record'. Corbin and Strauss (2008: 28) suggest that there are two possible reasons why this may occur. One is that the interviewee may be having some reflections or afterthoughts based on what they had said in the interview that do not emerge until after they believe it to be finished. The other is that the recorder might actually inhibit the interviewee from disclosing particular bits of information that they feel more comfortable to disclose once the recording is over. In these situations, the interviewer can of course ask whether the interviewee minds if they write down these afterthoughts so that they still have a record of them.

Another common occurrence at this stage is that the interviewee asks about how their answers compare to those provided by others. My experience of this is that they are both interested in receiving some reassurances that their contributions have been useful and interesting, and keen to see how their views fit with others. Here, the researcher can offer some commentary on what their initial interpretations of the research findings are. More complicated and another regular occurrence is when the interviewee asks who else is being interviewed for the research. Clearly here, the interviewer has a responsibility to protect the confidentiality of other informants and not disclose their names, but also to give some indication to the interviewee that appropriate others have been involved.

POST-INTERVIEW

After the interview, the task is to prepare the data for analysis. Before this can occur, there are some other potential issues to address. If you have recorded the interview, then the data will need to be transcribed. If you have conducted the interview in a language other than that required by your university for your dissertation, then there will also be translation issues to address.

Transcribing the interviews

One of the truisms of conducting qualitative research is that transcription is a laborious process that always takes far longer than initially expected. Given this, my advice is always to start to transcribe interviews as soon as you have done each one, rather than waiting until the whole set is complete. Otherwise, the task becomes even more daunting. Although there have been various developments in voice recognition software, the technology is still not at the stage where audio recordings can be translated directly into text with the level of accuracy required for data analysis. However, there are a number of tips that can save you some time as you approach this stage of analysis. Saunders et al. (2012) provide a useful checklist for transcription. The first point they make is that it is important that the transcription style is suitable for your choice of analytic technique. Another consideration here is whether the researcher will be using a software package such as NVivo to help the data analysis process. In this case, the form of transcription and the word-processing package required will need to be compatible. It is also useful to save each interview in a separate file as this makes the transfer of data into software packages somewhat easier.

Another tip from Saunders et al. (2012) is to ensure that you use appropriate respondent identifiers as part of the transcription. It may be that you do not want to use the names of your respondents in file names, for example, but you need some way of ensuring that you know who said what. In writing up summaries of the data, you might want to draw on quotes from the interviewees and here you will need to detail which interviewee said what, albeit using pseudonyms to protect confidentiality. More generally, anonymity and confidentiality need to be protected throughout the transcription process. Files should be kept secure and safe back-ups should also be retained.

There are a number of different approaches to transcription. Oliver, Serovich and Mason (2005: 1273) highlight that 'transcription practices can be thought of in terms of a continuum with two dominant modes: naturalism, in which every utterance is described in as much detail as possible, and denaturalism in which idiosyncratic elements of speech (e.g. stutters, pauses, non-verbals, involuntary vocalizations) are removed'. These different modes tie in with the various demands of analytic strategies. Given the time restriction with a dissertation, it is unlikely that you will want to take the naturalistic approach and include everything in your transcription, unless you need the idiosyncratic aspects of speech for the analysis.

In summary, although transcription may seem a relatively straightforward process, in that we just write down what someone has said, Hammersley (2010) suggests that there are a number of decisions to be made as part of the process that are often neglected within the literature. As well as what to transcribe and whether or not to include silences or pauses and non-verbal elements, there are issues around how to capture who people are addressing their comments to in multi-party talk such as group interviews and how to appropriately label the speakers. He suggests that 'it is important to recognize the constructive work that goes into transcription' (Hammersley, 2010: 558). Therefore, the researcher needs to decide what form of transcription to use and why.

Language and translation

Many students conducting dissertations in business and management schools do not have English as a first language, yet many schools internationally require that dissertations be written in English. This therefore creates a range of dilemmas around translation. Temple and Young (2004) suggest that the dilemmas or otherwise surrounding translation are informed by the epistemological position of the researcher. From a positivist perspective, where seeing research as neutral and bias free is key, the emphasis is on having the 'correct' interpretation of the text, therefore an important concern is the accuracy of translation. From an interpretivist stance, language and language use are culturally and contextually located, therefore removing language from that context – which is what translation effectively does – creates a number of interesting issues about multiple meanings and interpretation. There is little advice within the research methodology literature for those who need to translate as part of their data collection or data analysis process, suffice to say that a consideration of the impact that translation has on the knowledge produced is useful to include within the dissertation.

In order to understand some of the dilemmas that interviewers may face in regard to translation, it is worth reading some of the reflexive accounts of those who have used translation as part of their research. For example, Xian (2008: 232) suggests that the 'current understanding of data translation seems to be predominantly underpinned by positivist assumptions that there can be objective accounts existing between languages, and that a translator has nothing but technical rules'. In discussing her own experience of translating from Mandarin to English, Xian argues that translation is rather more of a messy process, which involves a degree of analysis and interpretation. There may be linguistic differences between languages where some words and phrases are not that easy to translate. Second, there are socio-cultural issues where idioms, metaphors and phrases used in China may not make sense to the English reader. Third, there are methodological issues – for example, whether the response from the reader in the original culture appropriates to the response from the reader in the target culture. As she suggests: 'translation is first a sensemaking exercise' (Xian, 2008: 240), requiring a reflexive approach.

Checking back with the interviewee

In some cases, the researcher may choose to go back to the interviewee after the interview to seek their views about what emerges from the research process. As with the other options outlined here, the key issue is that the researcher has a clear rationale for doing so. Some researchers, for example, promise to send the transcripts of an individual interview back to the interviewee for their comments. The question here is the purpose of doing this. The intention could be to ask them to check the accuracy of the transcript, but this seems a little unnecessary given that an audio recording should present a relatively accurate record, as long as it has been transcribed appropriately. Another approach could be to ask the interviewee to confirm that they are happy with what they said during the interview. This raises the issue of what the interviewer does with an interview where the interviewee suggests they are not happy afterwards. A more often used strategy is to go back to interviewees once the analysis has been done and the data has been interpreted to ask them for their views on the findings. This form of respondent validation or member checking is seen as a potential indicator of the validity of qualitative research. Indeed, Bryman and Bell (2007: 411) suggest that this is particularly popular amongst qualitative researchers because they are keen to see some correspondence between their own interpretations of the data and the perspectives of their respondents. However, the issue here is again the purpose of such respondent validation. What, for example, does the researcher do if their interpretations are challenged by the interviewee and a number of alternative interpretations provided? It is important that the researcher has a strategy for dealing with the outcomes of such an exercise.

BEYOND THE PRACTICALITIES: THE ACTIVE NATURE OF THE INTERVIEW

In our consideration of the interview so far, we have understood it as a fairly straightforward process where both parties know what to expect and the emphasis is on the interviewer gaining information from the interviewee through skilful questioning. However, the danger in treating the interview in this unproblematic way is that we forget that the interview is a social interaction. To this extent, we can see it as active, in that both interviewer and interviewee can lead its direction, and may both be interpreting what is happening in the interview in quite different ways. Within the literature on qualitative research, there has been an increased focus on the interview as an interactive process where meaning is co-constructed (e.g. Holstein and Gubrium, 1995; Denzin, 2001). This approach has more resonance with some ontological positions than others, most notably social constructionist approaches. Within this framework, the interview is seen as an arena where both interviewer and interviewee are actively constructing and interpreting the process. For example, Denzin suggests that 'interviews are performance texts' (2001: 27), which implies that as an interviewer we are seeking to perform in a particular role, the successful performance of which is an active accomplishment.

The performative nature of the interview: identity work

One way to consider the performative effects of the interview has been to focus on the nature of the 'identity work' that both interviewers and interviewees do as part of the interview process (e.g. Alvesson, 2003; Cassell, 2005; Collinson, 2006). Identity work, as defined by Sveningsson and Alvesson (2003), can be seen as a set of active processes which serve to construct a sense of identity. Here, we are not seeing identity as something static but rather as an ongoing process, hence the focus turns to understanding how interviews entail identity work by both the interviewer and the interviewee. Readers may be wondering why this is important in an interview situation so an example might help here. In discussing identity work, it is useful to start with a question that I am regularly asked by my students: 'What do I do if I know that the interviewee is not telling me the truth?' The issue is what we should do in this situation. It may be that we have direct evidence that someone is lying and we can gently probe their views about why other evidence may lead to alternative interpretations. However, one answer to the question above is that just because someone may not be telling the truth, this does not mean that what they say is not interesting for our research. Rapley (2001) suggests that there are a number of different issues that the analyst can assess in relation to identity work within the interview. For example, he argues that the identity work of the interviewer and interviewees should be a 'central part of the analysis' (2001: 304). So here we would ask ourselves why the interviewee needs to tell us this version of events. How are they explaining themselves here and what do they seek to achieve by talking in this particular way? This would be an interesting part of the analysis in Rapley's terms. Identity work is not just about what to do if someone may not be telling us what we think is the truth, but is about how the interviewee is working on constructing or performing their identity more generally.

Rapley (2001: 304) also argues that there should be an awareness and analysis of the function of the interviewer's talk in 'producing both the form and the content of the interview'. So this turns our attention to the identity work of the interviewer and how we as interviewers seek to construct our own identities as part of the interview process. We will be working to present ourselves as professional, competent and knowledgeable about the subject and as good interviewers, but that does take some work. It is also an interactive process so both interviewer and interviewee are not constructing their own identities in isolation but rather co-constructing them together throughout the interview, hence the active nature of the interview.

Drawing attention to identity work highlights how contextual aspects of the inter-view are important. For example, those researchers who focus on organizational story-telling (e.g. Boje, 1991; Gabriel and Griffiths, 2004) are interested in aspects of context that lead to the production of stories in interviews. Ylijoki (2005: 562), in her research on academic nostalgia, notes that 'an interview represents a special story-telling context', and she outlines what the characteristics of that context may be. In particular, compared to stories gathered as part of day-to-day organizational occurrences, the interview enables a story teller to reflect on their account as they proceed, which, Ylijoki argues, may enhance the quality of the stories recol-lected. So, in terms of interviewing for the dissertation, it is useful to consider what identity work both you and the interviewee may be doing as part of the interview process and why.

The role of the interviewer and reflexivity

In seeing the interview as active, the focus should not just be on the interviewee but also turn to the interviewer's performance. This draws attention to issues of reflexiv-ity (Johnson and Duberley, 2003; Alvesson and Sköldberg, 2011). Although there are different definitions of reflexivity within the literature, Haynes (2012: 72) suggests:

> in simple terms, reflexivity is an awareness of the researcher's role in the prac-tice of research and the way this is influenced by the object of the research, enabling the researcher to acknowledge the way in which he or she affects both the research processes and outcomes.

There are numerous examples within the management and organizational literature of this kind of approach. For example, writers such as Haynes (2006) have analysed the interviews they have conducted from a reflexive position, examining how gender has an impact on the organizational interviewing process. Bryman and Cassell (2006) produced a reflexive account of researcher interviews – where researchers interview other researchers – focusing on how the sense-making processes of both interviewer and interviewee are influenced by their assumed understanding of the purpose and aims of research interviews. Similarly, where interviewers have interviewed other academics, they have reflected on the dynamics of the process. For example, Ylijoki (2005: 562) outlined how both interviewer and interviewee are 'inhabitants' of the same territory, which can lead to an assumption of 'shared tacit knowledge'. This kind of recognition is important if your research project is focused within your own organization or the interviewees are similar to yourself.

One way of developing reflexive practice is through use of a research diary. Although the time spent on your dissertation will pass very quickly, I would strongly encourage you to create a diary of your interview research. Such a diary not only enables you to trace your own development, but also, as the researcher, you are an important instrument of data collection. Keeping a research diary is an important part of the research process. It enables you to jot down your thoughts as your research plans develop and to monitor your own learning. Furthermore, the diary can also be used as data. As a researcher, you are always collecting data, albeit of an informal nature. My experience suggests that students have also found their diaries useful in the final write-up of their dissertation. It can help you remember why your interview study went in a particular direction or why a methodological choice was made at a particular time. Referring back to the thoughts and reading that were associated with those choices is also useful. The diary can be in any format. It could be relatively unstructured, for example just a basic notebook that you make comments in when you can, or something more structured. A more structured diary may have, for example, entries on a weekly basis under different headings, such as *reading*, *methods* or *practical issues*. The key point is to find a format that suits you and your working style.

Power dynamics in the interview

A concern that has also received increasing attention in the literature is the power dynamics in the interview situation. This is a key theme that is dissected in the reflexive accounts referred to above. The nature of the power relationship within the interview setting is one that continues to concern many social science researchers (e.g. Denzin and Lincoln, 2005; Kvale, 2006). In some of these accounts, particularly those from an emancipatory perspective, the interviewer is presented as being in a powerful position in the role of expert who may indeed exploit the interviewee by taking their knowledge and giving little back. Kvale (2006: 483), for example, argues that the interview is inevitably a hierarchical encounter and that the 'power dynamics in research interviews, and potential oppressive use of interview-produced knowledge, tend to be left out in literature on qualitative research'. However, there is also the situation within much of business and management research where interviewees may be in a more powerful position than the researcher by virtue of their organizational position. Given this, there is now a considerable literature about interviewing organizational elites, and the dilemmas that may be involved (e.g. Zuckerman, 1972; Kezar, 2003; Conti and O'Neill, 2007; Stephens, 2007). Harvey (2011) points out that the issues with elites are not necessarily that different from other interview contexts, but there may be particularities in these kinds of interviews which are important to consider.

Individual characteristics of the interviewer and the interviewee such as gender, age and ethnicity are also important here (e.g. Lawthom, 1998; Cassell, 2005) and a consideration of these can be found in the reflexive accounts of interviewers. Lawthom (1998), for example, discusses some of the power relationships at work in her interviews with managers in the manufacturing industry and highlights that as a relatively young woman interviewing older men a number of metaphors characterized the interviews as she experienced them. These ranged from feeling that the interview was some kind of sexual liaison to a form of parent-child interaction, in each case with her being in the less powerful position.

There are also other ways in which interviews can be sites for power struggles. For example, Tanggaard (2007: 162) outlines how in her interviews with apprentices about their vocational learning, the interview could meaningfully be seen as a 'battlefield', where competing discourses about the value of vocational learning came into play. She argues that although the direct struggle for power may not always be evident within an interview setting, the ongoing negotiation of meaning is evidence of a power struggle which may in itself encourage the interviewer to reflect more thoroughly on their own assumptions with regard to question asking.

Predictability of the interview process

First-time interviewers often highlight that what surprises them the most is the lack of predictability in the interview encounter. Understanding the interview as an active process gives us a framework for realizing why this is the case. However, with the different types of semi-structured interviews outlined in Chapter 2, it may be that there is room for manoeuvre as the interview progresses. If new issues emerge as more interviews are conducted, then there is no reason why these cannot be followed up in later interviews. Within the research literature, there are accounts that critique both the desirability and likelihood of the researcher sticking to traditional interview protocols. For example, McCabe (2007: 248), in discussing his interviews in an automobile manufacturing plant, explicitly states that the research was 'emergent' and progressed in line with his intuition during the 'extensive period of interviewing'. Therefore, the idea of a predictable interview based on set procedures is seen as inappropriate in this kind of research where the research question may be evolving. Having said that, given the time constraints on a dissertation, it is important that there are some boundaries around the research question and the interview topic so that the dissertation will be completed on time. The point here is to reassure the reader that despite the ordered account of research that is often expressed in journal articles, the process can be a bit more complex and messy (see Donnelly et al., 2013). As Learmonth (2006: 94) suggests, 'With research interviews (as with other parts of our lives) there is always an undecidability that disables mastery'. By implication, the interviewer can never be fully prepared for what might arise. Although these types of debates focus more on qualitative interviews than on more structured quantitative approaches, they serve to remind organizational researchers that the research interview can be unpredictable and sometimes produce the unexpected.

ETHICAL ISSUES IN INTERVIEWING

As mentioned earlier, it is important that the interviewer behaves in what is considered an ethical manner. Student research is increasingly subject to ethical regulation which is a characteristic of the increased significance of ethical regulation within the field more generally (e.g. Bryman and Bell, 2007; Buchanan and Bryman, 2007), and the majority of textbooks about interviewing focus on some of the ethical issues involved with the process. Your own university will have a set of guidelines about the conduct of ethical research which you must adhere to. You may also need some form of ethical clearance from a university committee before you have permission to conduct the work, and if you want to work with particular groups, such as with children or in the British National Health Service (NHS), there are additional extensive processes for ethical approval that you will need to go through. Indeed, it may be that the length of time required to achieve ethical approval for your research design prohibits a consideration of working in certain locations such as the NHS.

Depending on the content of your degree, you will also be expected to meet the ethical codes of the relevant professional associations. For example, if your degree is in Marketing you will be expected to adhere to the ethical code of the Market Research Society (see www.mrs.org.uk/standards/code_of_conduct/). An organizational psychologist in the UK will be expected to conduct their research in the context of the British Psychological Society (see www.bps.org.uk/what-we-do/ethics-standards/ethics-standards). Other professional associations, such as the British Sociological Association and the Chartered Institute of Personnel and Development, also have such codes. The content of these codes is fairly similar in that researchers should ensure that they seek informed consent for the research and that no harm should come to research participants, either to them personally or to their organizations, for example through the disclosure of commercially sensitive data. The interviewer should be familiar with what is seen to be good ethical practice so that they can implement it throughout their study. A common question asked is what happens to overseas students who may be, for example, registered for a degree in one country yet conduct their interviews in another? Different countries have different regulations about interviewing certain vulnerable groups. The advice is that the interviewer should conform to the ethical code of the university where they are registered for their degree, as the university has a responsibility to ensure that their research meets the demands of ethical practice. Box 4.3 provides an example of a professional association ethical code of conduct.

4.3 Market Research Society ethical code of conduct

There are many different types of ethical codes for research conduct. This one comes from the Market Research Society (see www.mrs.org.uk/standards/code_of_conduct/).

These are the principles of the MRS Code of Conduct:

1. Researchers shall ensure that participation in their activities is based on voluntary informed consent.
2. Researchers shall be straightforward and honest in all their professional and business relationships.
3. Researchers shall be transparent as to the subject and purpose of data collection.
4. Researchers shall respect the confidentiality of information collected in their professional activities.
5. Researchers shall respect the rights and well-being of all individuals.
6. Researchers shall ensure that respondents are not harmed or adversely affected by their professional activities.
7. Researchers shall balance the needs of individuals, clients and their professional activities.
8. Researchers shall exercise independent professional judgement in the design, conduct and reporting of their professional activities.
9. Researchers shall ensure that their professional activities are conducted by persons with appropriate training, qualifications and experience.
10. Researchers shall protect the reputation and integrity of the profession.

It is useful to see issues of ethics as pertinent to all stages of the research process, not just in the conduct of the interview. So, there are also considerations around how the analysis of interview data is presented. For example, in relation to narrative interviews, Gabriel and Griffiths (2004: 124), when discussing the interpretation of organizational stories, caution against assuming that stories as presented are fact. They suggest that 'stories are especially pernicious because of their memorable qualities. As every journalist knows, through selective presentation, editing, highlighting and framing, a narrative may be put to work within virtually any overall story'. Therefore, how we choose to represent an organization or individual through our reporting is a sensitive issue that it is important to give some thought to.

RESEARCHING YOUR OWN ORGANIZATION

There are a number of reasons why dissertation students conduct research in organizations they are familiar with. It may be that you are conducting research in your own organization because they are sponsoring your degree. Or it may be that a student has secured access to a company that they have previously worked in. Interviewing in your own organization causes a particular set of ethical and reflexive dilemmas that need attending to. The interviewees may be quite familiar to the interviewer but they are not used to the interviewer being in the role of researcher. Hence, boundaries around the research and the interviewer's role can be muddy and imprecise. This can create difficulties for both sides. Tietze (2012) suggests that it is important to reflect on the roles of the researcher and the researched in this kind of context. For example, in these cases the research will be informed by the knowledge the interviewer already has of the organization and the interviewees. It is important that this is acknowledged and accounted for in any interpretation of the interviews. Tietze (2012) produces some guidelines for qualitative researchers who are conducting research in their own organizations which are useful to consider if you find yourself in this situation.

CONCLUSIONS

Within this chapter, we have drawn attention to both the practicalities and some of the complexities that are involved in research interviewing. In seeing the interview as an active process which is co-constructed by both the interviewer and the interviewee, issues of power and identity and the need for reflexivity are brought to the fore. This view of the interview is informed by a social constructionist approach and the issues outlined are less likely to be identified in research designs where the interview is highly structured and informed by a positivist stance. Here, the intention would be to minimize the influence of these complicating factors. A key question the reader may ask is, what do I do about these issues? Being reflexive is about being aware of the researcher role and therefore we should show that we have noted issues such as identity processes at work within our dissertation. Some researchers write a separate brief reflexive account at the end of the dissertation that considers the things we have noted here.

Having made the comment about a social constructionist perspective leading us to a focus on these complexities, it should be said that it is important to recognize that taking an ethical approach to interviewing and being guided by an appropriate ethical code is crucial regardless of the epistemological stance. This is also a key criterion on which the examiner will be assessing your research, which we will again return to in Chapter 6.

5

EXAMPLES OF RESEARCH INTERVIEWS

INTRODUCTION

The aim of this chapter is to provide some more detailed illustrations of how interviews are used in the business, organization and management literature. In outlining some of the published work where interviews are used, we return to the framework of different types of interviews provided in Table 2.1 and consider uses of structured, semi-structured and unstructured interviews.

STRUCTURED INTERVIEWS

Structured interviews have been used within the business, management and organizational literature in a number of different ways. In Table 2.1, they are divided into interviews where the aim is to gather information and those where the aim is to test hypotheses. We now address each of these in turn.

Structured interviews: information gathering

The use of structured interviews for information gathering is a popular approach within business and management research. An example can be found in Cassell et al. (2002) who used two types of interview methods to study the kinds of human resource management (HRM) practices used by small and medium-sized enterprises (SMEs). The research questions for the study were: What HR practices are used by SMEs? To what extent are these practices seen as effective in achieving their objectives? What characterizes the use of HR practices in the SME? As we noted earlier, a structured interview and a questionnaire are fairly similar and Cassell et al. (2002) describe their telephone interviews as a survey. The aim of the telephone interview or survey was to examine the extent to which a range of HRM practices were used by the companies the authors were interested in. The authors designed the interview instrument and then a market research company conducted the telephone interviews. Using random sampling from the population of companies that fitted into the definition of an SME, 100 senior managers from SMEs were interviewed. The response rate of those invited to interview was 56 per cent. These structured telephone interviews enabled the collection of data to address the question of what practices the firms were using and the extent to which they were using them. To answer the questions of why and how they were using them, the authors conducted semi-structured face-to-face interviews with senior managers from 22 SMEs in the target population. This part of the study addressed the same questions but also asked questions about recent changes to HR practices in the company and the reasons for these changes; how those change processes were managed; and any future changes planned. This enabled a far more detailed investigation of what was happening in practice. Therefore, this study is an example of how structured interviews for information gathering can be used with semi-structured interviews in the same research project. From their findings, the authors devised a model of the characteristics that influence whether an SME adopts a particular HR policy or otherwise, and the authors conclude that current business priorities are a more likely indicator of whether an SME will adopt an HR practice than a strategic approach.

A further example comes from the field of strategy where Alexander, Meising and Parsons (2005) ask the research question: How important are stakeholder relationships? Here, the researchers used structured interviews as part of a mixed methods design which was in two data collection phases. At the initial stage of the research, it was important for the researchers to understand the nature of stakeholder relationships and how they developed over time. They created three panels of interviewees who represented various areas of the economy, for example banking, pharmaceutical and non-profit-making organizations. During this first phase, structured interviews took place with members of top management teams of those organizations. The authors outline that they used a 'standardised open-ended interview' where all interviewees were asked exactly the same questions in the same way in the same order (Alexander et al., 2005: 4). The choice to use structured interviews in this way was to ensure that the process was systematic. The authors point out that it also made the data analysis somewhat easier in that the data could be quantified. The authors also took a novel approach and had a series of open-ended questions where respondents could comment on additional issues that they perceived to be important in their relationships with their stakeholders. As the authors point out in the article: 'These questions were designed to explore the relationships the members of the top management groups have with their stakeholders and to generate items for the survey instrument' (Alexander et al., 2005: 4). The types of questions in these interviews mainly focused on asking respondents to describe their experiences of stakeholder relationships in the present and the past. The authors conclude, amongst other things, that providing a good service means there is a greater likelihood of an exchange relationship continuing. Therefore, this study is an example of how a structured interview format can be used as an exploratory tool where the findings can be fed into the design of the next stage of the research: in this case, a survey.

Structured interviews: hypothesis testing

The use of structured interviews also enables the testing of hypotheses, something that it is difficult to achieve when using semi-structured interviews. Again, this is a well-used approach within management research. One example from the field of social entrepreneurship comes from Zhang and Swanson (2013). In their study, they were interested in investigating the research question of how non-profit organizations (NPOs) manage their business and social objectives. Therefore, they designed a number of hypotheses based on the literature and previous evidence, including 'Employing multiple non-financial measures enhances NPOs' performance outcomes' and 'The more social value a NPO delivers, the more likely it will self-identify as being social entrepreneurial' (Zhang and Swanson, 2013: 112-13). In order to test these and other hypotheses, the authors used a structured interview schedule which was initially piloted with 30 community leaders who provided useful feedback on the measure. In terms of standardizing the data within the interview, some of the questions used four-point Likert scales, for example about the extent to which the organizations employed business or social objectives in their missions. A final sample comprised of 202 interviewees. Where structured interview schedules like this are used, it is usual to have a far larger sample than with semi-structured approaches. This is also required to enable hypothesis testing. The authors conclude by suggesting that the quantitative analysis of their interview data offers reliable and significant support for the findings within the literature previously established through qualitative research, thereby highlighting the advantages of being able to quantitatively analyse interview data.

A further example comes from the work of Paul and Rana (2013) who aimed to investigate a research question about the purchasing intentions of ecological consumers in relation to organic foods. They were particularly interested in what factors influenced consumer behaviour towards organic food. The hypotheses they generated from the literature review included 'Consumers purchase organic food for the health benefits' and 'Availability is important for choosing organic food' (Paul and Rana, 2013: 414). In order to test these hypotheses, amongst others, the researchers designed a structured questionnaire that was used in 301 face-to-face interviews. The questions in the survey included demographic questions and those about the availability of organic food and the reasons for buying it. Convenience sampling was used so customers were approached as they were leaving stores and asked if they were prepared to take part in the interviews. The structured nature and the volume of data collected enabled the authors to test their hypotheses and conclude from the study that healthy content was the most important thing on consumers' minds. This research design demonstrates that again structured interview schedules are very similar to questionnaires and therefore have the same advantages in terms of being able to test hypotheses through the use of clearly operationalized variables.

As well as the testing of hypotheses, structured interview schedules also enable the direct testing of theory. For example, McNamee and McHugh (1989) used Porter's competitive framework to assess the competitiveness of the Northern Ireland garment industry. Testing the theory involved operationalizing the complex dimension of competitiveness on three complementary measures: net profit before tax, sales per employee and sales per pound of assets. They operationalized the framework by analysing at both industry and strategic group level. Face-to-face interviews were then held with 77 different clothing firms. The amount of standardized data that came from using a structured interview format enabled the authors to conclude that 'This study appears to show that the work of Michael Porter is a worthwhile and practical methodology for investigating sectoral and individual firm competitiveness' (McNamee and McHugh, 1989: 70).

These examples highlight how within the field more generally, structured interviews are used to enable the standardization of the data collected so that it can be quantitatively analysed and theory can be tested.

SEMI-STRUCTURED INTERVIEWS: THEMATIC FORMAT

Semi-structured interviews provide the researcher with a range of different options and focus more on the qualitative analysis of interview data. Here, we return to the different types of semi-structured interviews referred to in Chapter 2 and look at some examples.

Exploratory interviews

Within the literature, there are many different examples of how a semi-structured interview can be used to explore a particular phenomenon of interest. An example from the field of accounting comes from Gendron and Spira (2010). For their study into identity work, they conducted interviews with 25 people who had previously been members of the Arthur Anderson company in Canada and the UK. The researchers were interested in how the breakdown of the firm was understood by those who had previously worked for it. Nearly all of the interviews were conducted around two years after the firm's indictment by the US Department of Justice and the authors comment on how this meant that the interviewees had had considerable time to process and reflect on what had happened to the firm at that time. This example is particularly interesting because the data the authors were accessing was of a very sensitive nature and in their account of their study they talk about ways in which this sensitivity was managed. For example, they comment:

> We initially believed that interviewees would consider the topic investigated as highly sensitive. Our intuition was later confirmed through a number of participants who mentioned that they were very worried about the possibility of seeing in the public domain excerpts of their interview along with information that would allow others to identify them. In particular, one participant who provided extensive information about the collapse and his feelings about it, emphasized that he would not have participated had he not known one of the authors very well. (Gendron and Spira, 2010: 280)

The interviews were semi-structured and interviewees were encouraged to talk freely about the collapse of the company. The questions asked focused on the organizational background of the company; the reasons and consequences of what happened; and the interviewee's viewpoints about control mechanisms in accounting firms. The research team also used a number of practices to reassure the interviewees that it was safe to disclose information. These included guarantees of anonymity and confidentiality; the opportunity to verify the content of the transcript and make any changes at a later stage; the opportunity to comment on a draft of the published paper; and the lack of respondent identifiers in the final paper. From their research, the authors conclude that the processes of identity work are important in understanding how discourses circulate in society.

A second example of an exploratory semi-structured interview takes a very different approach and considers how semi-structured interviews can be used at the exploratory stage of a mixed methods project. Blumrodt, Bryson and Flanagan (2012) were interested in exploring the impact of European football teams' CSR engagement on customer-based brand equity. In their study, the focus was on customer perceptions of particular football clubs as brands and the impact of those perceptions on purchasing behaviour. An important aim of the study was to design a questionnaire to test these issues with a variety of football clubs. Therefore, interviews were used in the first stage of the study to explore the key issues that fans had that would need to be in the questionnaire. The authors chose two football clubs in which to do the research: *Stade Rennais*, which the authors describe as a regional brand with a chance of national recognition, and *Football Club de Lorient*, a local brand recently promoted to the First Division. Although the authors do not state how many interviews they conducted, they use the concept of data saturation – defined as interviewing until there was no new information being generated – to decide when to stop interviewing. The kinds of questions asked in the interview schedule were about different aspects of fan loyalty, including team performance, club values, playing style, and facilities. When examining the findings from the analysis, they noticed some interesting gender differences in the results in that: 'All interviewees mentioned the clubs' sporting performance, players' techniques and teams' tactics, while male respondents also raised the issue of general management skills. Female respondents were more prone to mention comfort and cleanliness of the facilities' (Blumrodt et al., 2012: 483). These findings were an important part of the research in that the authors suggest they provided the foundation for understanding the brand images and brand associations of customers which could then be fed into the fans' questionnaire. Hence, here the semi-structured interviews were used at an exploratory stage of the project as part of a mixed methods design. The authors concluded, amongst other things, that the football clubs should focus on more customer-focused communication.

The third example is different again and focuses on an exploratory interview study that sought to explore how globalization is impacting on women working in the accounting and finance professions in Syria. Kamla (2012) conducted 22 semi-structured interviews with female accountants in Syria. The interview questions focused on the women's experiences of the accounting and finance professions in Syria more generally. Kamla then transcribed and translated the interviews from Arabic to English, pointing out that she tried not to distort the meanings of the interviews during the translation process. The issue of translation is a difficult one, as we discussed in the previous chapter. One of the key issues that is addressed in the paper is the wearing of the hiqab by Muslim women. Kamla (2012) offers a reflexive approach in the article and outlines her own background, including her past work in Syria and her current location in the UK. She outlines how this

> helped her gain access to (and the trust of) the participants through shared experiences of working as an accountant and being a woman in Syria … the researcher, on meeting the interviewees for the first time, told them a bit about herself, her work and the purpose of her research in order to increase trust and build a rapport. (2012: 193)

As part of her reflexive stance, Kamla recognizes that 'some interviewees, however, might have perceived the researcher as "Westernized"; this may be true to some extent since she lives in the UK and does not wear a hijab; this may have influenced aspects of their answers'. (2012: 193)

Kamla (2012: 198) analyses her findings using discourse analysis and comes to the interesting conclusion that 'the issue of female clothing for Muslim women is still overemphasized in the East and West'. Her suggestion is that 'we need to go beyond the politics of the hijab and focus on addressing broader socio-political, cultural and global conditions that are contributing to Syrian women's marginalization in the accounting and finance professions and beyond' Kamla (2012: 188). Hence, the exploratory nature of the semi-structured interview enabled attention to be drawn to a distinctive aspect of Syrian women's experiences. In summary, each of the three examples highlight the variety that can be found in semi-structured exploratory interviews.

Theoretical interviews

Semi-structured interviews can also be used to investigate theory. Our first example comes from Dennis and Parkhe (2002) who were interested in devising theory in the area of Hungarian–Western business partnerships. In doing so, they were using interviews as part of a multiple case study design. In order to see how these international co-operative ventures worked, they conducted 17 case studies based on Yin's (1994) approach. From their literature review, the authors generated a series of propositions that they aimed to test through the case studies. To devise a sample, the research team identified who was the most senior manager for each of the venture partners. These individuals were then asked who would be the most suitable people to be interviewed. This is a useful approach when trying to find out who are the most appropriate informants to talk to within a company. This method of interviewee identification led to the team interviewing two to six managers for each case. The semi-structured interviews lasted about 90 minutes and the authors describe how they were the primary source of data for each case, though company documents and archival data were also collected systematically on each site to enable triangulation and the building of theory in the analytic process. The authors conclude that their methodology enables new insights in this area and helps to highlight how inter-firm relationships are complex. Hence, this is a good example of where semi-structured interviews can be used to build theory through case study analysis.

Another example of the role semi-structured interviews can play in case study research comes from Braunscheidel, Hamister, Suresh and Star (2010). Here, the authors were interested in using institutional theory to explore the motivations behind companies adopting Six Sigma methodologies and the consequent impact on the firm's performance. A series of propositions were designed from the literature that enabled the theoretical links to be explored through the data analysis. Six Sigma methodologies are operations management interventions similar to total quality initiatives but with an additional focus on performance. They have been defined in a number of ways including a disciplined approach and statistically based approach for improving product and process quality (Hahn et al., 1999). Individuals can attain different levels of capability and certification in Six Sigma methods, ranging from green belt to black belt, and the research team wanted to reflect this in their selection of interviewees. To address this, they devised what are described as both vertical and horizontal interviewee selection protocols. To gain an insight across all employees in a given company, different interviewees were identified at different levels – in effect, the company was divided vertically as part of the sampling strategy. The second interview protocol was referred to as a horizontal one where interviews were conducted with managers at the same level of the company hierarchy. As the authors outline:

> for example, if a master black belt was interviewed, the other interviewees could be either two black belts (horizontal relationship between the black belts), or one black belt and one person whose position is of a horizontal nature to the master black belt (e.g. VP operations). (Braunscheidel et al., 2010: 432)

This sampling strategy was again tied into the desire to achieve triangulation within the case study design. One-hour-long interviews were conducted with 26 people. Another interesting aspect of this research was that two interviewers were used for each interview – one to ask questions and one to take notes. As the authors comment: 'employment of a two-person research team may enable the team to establish different perspectives of the case. The interviewer can establish a more personal relationship with the interviewee while the data recorder maintains a more distant view' (Braunscheidel et al., 2010: 433). The results from the interviews were used to test the propositions as part of the overall case study design. From their study, the authors concluded that organizations that adopted Six Sigma are able to satisfy their customers.

A somewhat different example of the use of semi-structured interviews in relation to theory comes from the field of finance. Willman, Fenton-O'Creevy, Nicholson and Soane (2006) were interested in challenging the efficient markets hypothesis in finance that the markets work in an efficient manner based on the information available at any given time. Their argument was that this hypothesis cannot explain the high levels of trading that occur and that there must be some irrationality in the process. Hence, the researchers designed a multi-methods study to consider how irrationality could be understood, given that it is insufficiently explained in the literature. The authors conducted semi-structured interviews with 118 traders about a range of different issues and asked questions about their experiences of trading, such as their motivations, emotions and experiences of gain and loss. The qualitative findings from these hour-long interviews were analysed alongside quantitative data from a personality questionnaire and a test of cognitive bias. The authors conclude from their research that whereas from within the efficient markets hypothesis 'the existence of noise trading ostensibly shows large scale irrational risk', they would argue that 'for traders it is a necessary form of risk exposure. Frequent trading allows traders opportunities for learning, sensation seeking, information search and network building' (Willman et al., 2006: 1371). Hence, the use of semi-structured interviews in this study enables an alternative interpretation of the role of noise within the efficient markets hypothesis to be understood.

SEMI-STRUCTURED INTERVIEWS: DISTINCTIVE FORMAT

We now turn to semi-structured interviews where there is a distinctive structure or format, starting with event-based interviews.

Event-based interviews

The most common form of event-based interviews is those based on critical incident technique (CIT). One example comes from Speakman and Ryals (2012) who were interested in how key sales account managers handled multiple incidences of simultaneous conflict whilst carrying out their own internal selling duties. The authors conducted interviews with 29 key account managers across seven international organizations within the fast-moving consumer goods (FMCG) market. For this study, the critical incident was defined as an internal conflict. As with other CIT studies, the interviewees made their own judgements about what these conflicts – or critical incidents – were. The authors describe the processes for generating the incidents:

> Each respondent was asked to recollect, in their own words, two types of incidents, those which were effectively resolved or mitigated, and those which were ineffectively resolved or agitated. Through open questions each participant was asked to recollect the skills and behaviours adopted in the management of these conflict incidents and their perceptions of the outcome. (Speakman and Ryals, 2012: 363)

The authors conclude that whilst previous research has shown how salespeople need to change their behaviours and interaction when working on sales externally to the organization, they also need to do the same internally when managing conflict in the organization; indeed, 'conflict is a constant and inherent condition of key account management within the organization' (Speakman and Ryals, 2012: 369).

Another example of the CIT in use comes from Chell (2004), who was interested in exploring the internal dynamics of the micro-business household to look at the interaction between work and family and the implications of that for work and family. Chell (2004) talks in detail about how to plan the CIT; how to focus on a theme throughout; and the generic probes that accompany the incident. These can include: What happened next? Why did it happen? How did it happen? With whom did it happen? What did the parties concerned feel? What were the consequences – immediately and longer term? How did the respondent cope? (Chell, 2004: 49). Such questions help to structure the CIT interview and also enable access to understanding the set-up of the business from the owner's perspective. Therefore, structuring the interview in this way is a useful way of encouraging the interviewee to talk at length.

Comparative interviews

When discussing comparative interviews in Chapter 2, the key example offered was the repertory grid based on Kelly's personal construct theory. An interesting account of a repertory grid interview is provided by Langan-Fox and Tan (1997). Here, the repertory grid was used as a part of a two-stage mixed methods study that was investigating change and stability in organizational culture in an organization that had moved from a public service orientation to a customer service orientation.

The in-depth interviews that formed the basis of the repertory grid part of the study were conducted with 13 middle managers. The authors provide a useful example of how to explain to interview participants how the repertory grid works through the comparison process by providing interviewees with examples of how they might compare a car, a tram and a donkey as forms of transport. Through making these comparisons, they bring out some of the key procedures of the repertory grid process, for example that there are different combinations of elements where bipolar descriptions are required. After providing these illustrative examples, the authors then explain that the interviewees will be asked to go through a similar process but with people they know. In this study, the elements for the elicitation of constructs included a staff member who could be considered 'typical'; another staff member who could be considered 'less typical'; a unit/team manager who could be considered 'typical'; a unit/team manager who could be considered 'less typical'; and someone typical of senior management (see Langan-Fox and Tan, 1997). The standardized triads for eliciting the constructs are then presented. The aim was to elicit the content of the organizational culture through this repertory grid process, and once the interviews were complete the constructs generated were content analysed to generate five main ways in which the old culture contrasted with the new culture. As noted previously, this was a mixed methods study and the interview findings led to the creation of a survey that was then distributed throughout the organization. Hence, the repertory grid interview in this case was used as a way of facilitating the collection of quantitative data at a later stage.

Another example of a repertory grid study is provided by Cassell and Walsh (2004), who were interested in the behaviours that were seen as effective for progression into senior management levels in the publishing industry. The methods for the study were repertory grid interviews with 60 male and female managers at four different publishing companies. Eleven different elements were used for construct elicitation that represented key characters in an individual's work and home lives. The elements included a competent manager at work; an incompetent manager at work; a female work colleague; someone who supports me at work; and myself. In each case, interviewees were told to think of the same person in each of these categories when the construct was used, though they were not to tell the interviewer who it was they were thinking of. Once the grid was completed, interviewees were asked to mark on the grid on a scale of 1 to 7 the extent to which a behaviour was important for them to do a good job and, second, the extent to which they thought each behaviour led to success in the company. An example of a complete repertory grid from this study is shown in Box 5.1.

Box 5.1   Example of a completed repertory grid (from Cassell and Walsh, 2004: 65)

In control	*		X					Out of control
Accessible		X			*			Untrustworthy/ impersonal
Mild in views			X				*	Dominant and forceful
Self-confident	*						X	Lacking in confidence
Concerned with people around them		X			*			No concern with their impact on others
Ambitious in career	*			X				Unambitious
Impulsive/ill-considered						*	X	Objective and calm
High academic achievement		X	*					Solid, down to earth
Consistent achiever	*	X						Inconsistent achiever
Immense ambition		*		X				Comfortable with themselves

X The extent to which this behaviour is important for me to do a good job

• The extent to which this behaviour is important to be successful in the company

Therefore, in this case the grids generated in the interviews were used to identify any discrepancies between what was seen as important to do a good job and what the company rewarded. The different conceptualizations that men and women had of these issues could also be explored.

Narrative interviews

A further kind of semi-structured interview is the narrative interview. There is considerable flexibility in how narrative interviews work so here we talk through two different examples. The first study, by Vaara (2002), focuses on how organizational members make sense of the success or failure of post-merger integration which draws on extensive interview material from eight Finnish-Swedish mergers. The interviewees for this study were key organizational actors who had been closely involved in the merger processes and the author describes how a story-telling approach was used for interviewing. This meant that in the interview the interviewees were asked to recount their experiences of the integration processes and to tell their stories about how they had experienced things post-merger. Vaara (2002) describes an important process of qualitative interviewing that is often unacknowledged in the literature: 'the specific questions I asked and the themes that were brought up varied from interview to interview as my knowledge of the cases increased and as my empirical research questions evolved' (Vaara, 2002: 222). The interviews usually lasted between two and three hours and the data were analysed through a focus on the discourses that underpinned the stories told. Conclusions from the study overall include the interesting outcome that success stories tend to lead to over-optimistic views of the amount of control that managers have over the change process, whereas failure stories lead to over-pessimistic accounts.

Hamilton (2006) takes a different approach to consider the stories told by founders of family businesses and their families about their experiences of working together in the family business. Hamilton states how the narrative interviews began with 'a range of conversational devices such as "tell me about the family and the business" or "where did it all begin?"' (2006: 540). She outlines how these types of open questions encourage interviewees to tell their own stories. From these kinds of narrative interviews, data are generated about the rich interplay between different generations of family members and the narratives produced are critiqued in relation to the different literary genres such as epic, tragedy and comedy.

Hence, the focus of narrative interviews on the stories that interviewees tell, provides an alternative way of conducting a semi-structured interview.

Biographical interviews

There are some similarities between biographical and narrative interviews in that both focus on the interviewee telling their story, though for a biographical interview the focus is on their life story. Therefore, questions in the interview schedule will focus on the different stages and experiences of an interviewee's life. Cohen and Mallon (2001) draw on stories as a tool but do so within a biographical interview. They highlight how within the field of career research, the story is seen as a useful tool, in that people tend to tell stories of their careers. In this case, their interest was in workers who had made the transition to self-employment or portfolio working. They highlight how their experiences of conducting initial interviews showed that people liked to tell their stories in some form of chronological order, implying that such an important job move could not be seen as abstract or separate from their career development more generally or from aspects of their non-working lives. As the authors outline: 'the transition from employment to portfolio work thus became an episode in a respondent's overall life/career story, an episode that was seen to make sense in terms of this unfolding narrative' (Cohen and Mallon, 2001: 55). This work is especially interesting in drawing attention to how a particular form of interview may be more appropriate for a particular research question. So here, where the emphasis is on significant personal change, a method that can account for temporal aspects of experience is useful.

A different example of a narrative approach comes from Roberts (2002) who, in exploring the nature of Board effectiveness, interviewed 35 company chairs, chief executives and non-executive directors from FTSE 100 companies. The interviews lasted about 90 minutes and sought to trace their experiences of working in these different roles. Given that the interviewees were in a number of these roles at some point in their career, a biographical approach was appropriate in that the interviews focused on the interlinkages between the different roles at different times in their lives. The author concludes by suggesting that the role of non-executives is to support and complement the work of executives. In this study, a biographical approach is not explicitly taken but emerges again as a result of the questions that are asked.

Visual techniques

There are a range of different visual techniques that can be used in interviews. Here, we will look at two examples of how visual techniques can be used within a semi-structured interview. Mazzetti and Blenkinsopp (2012) were interested to see how visual methods could be used within the area of stress research which is typically informed by quantitative methods. In order to explore the stresses associated with career change, they conducted semi-structured interviews with 16 volunteers who were told that the only output of the interview would be a visual timeline. Each of the interviews lasted approximately two hours and during that period interviewees were asked to draw a timeline that commenced from when they first started to think about their own careers to the present time. The creation of the timeline progressed through the interview with them identifying key transitions and relevant life events. As the authors (Mazzetti and Blenkinsopp, 2012: 653) outline, 'participants were encouraged to use imagery, in the forms of emoticons (happy faces for positively appraised events; sad faces for negatively appraised events), visual metaphors or drawings'. Throughout the interview, both interviewer and interviewee discussed the timeline and the meanings associated with the various drawings and symbols. Hence, the end product was a rich pictorial representation of the interviewee's view of their own career transition process. The authors concluded from this research that understanding coping with stress requires a historical context.

A different form of visual methods is the use of photographs within interviews. These can either be shown to interviewees for their comment or can be elicited from interviewees and discussed in the interview itself. Slutskaya, Simpson and Hughes (2012) argue that the use of photographs enables the discussion of issues about work with groups who may be less used to being engaged in such discussions. In their study drawing on photo-elicitation methods, before the interviews the participants were given digital cameras and asked to capture photographically what they saw to be key aspects of their work environment. In the interviews, the interviewees were then asked to talk about the photographs and therefore their work more generally. The research question for the study overall was how male workers experienced and accounted for dirty work. The authors highlight how within the interviews having the photographs meant that the men could talk about the physicality required for their work and be nostalgic about how that work had changed. The authors conclude that

> the use of photo-elicitation in the exploration of a class and gendered 'habitus' has highlighted the power of visual methods to offer a closer look at what participants considered important, to open space for the emergence of unexpected topics and themes and to allow for a more comprehensive and reflective elaboration on specialities of personal experiences and emotions. (Slutskaya et al., 2012: 16)

This opportunity to access such emotional understandings is seen to be one of the strengths of using visual methods within a semi-structured interview setting.

UNSTRUCTURED INTERVIEWS

Phenomenological interviews

When unstructured interviews were outlined in Chapter 2, phenomenological approaches were provided as an example. There are few studies within the business and management field that draw exclusively on unstructured phenomenological interviews, though one exception is Cope's work on researching entrepreneurship. Cope (2005) conducted phenomenological interviews with six practising entrepreneurs. Typically, the in-depth nature of unstructured interviews means that the sample sizes for such studies are usually quite small. As the author outlines, within these kinds of approaches the sampling is not intended to be representative but rather 'each participant was chosen for the unique and highly interesting story that they would bring to the research process' (Cope, 2005: 175). The aim of the phenomenological interview is to gain the interviewee's description of a phenomenon of interest. Therefore, the role of the interviewer is to 'provide a context in which participants feel free to describe their experiences in detail' (Cope, 2005: 176). Here, the only imposed structure on the interview is when the interviewee is told at the beginning about the focus of the research and the topic the interviewer is interested in. After that, the interviewee is just encouraged to talk as they would like. Clearly, this is a very flexible technique, although there is some element of risk for the less experienced researcher.

CONCLUSIONS

In this chapter, we have looked in more detail at some examples of the different types of interviews that are available to the researcher. Through these examples, we can see the extensive variety that the interview has to offer as a research method. We now turn to the advantages and disadvantages of using interviews and consider how to plan for what is required once our interviews are complete.

6

CONCLUSIONS

INTRODUCTION

In this final chapter, we first of all critique the research interview and then consider the next steps in the process by thinking ahead to analysing and writing up the interview data. We then conclude by summarizing the book overall.

CRITIQUING THE INTERVIEW

We have now covered all aspects of the interview process from beginning to end. In the following sections, we reflect on what a good interview looks like and the advantages and disadvantages of using interviews in a dissertation research project.

Advantages of the research interview

The dissertation researcher has a range of research methods available to them through which a research question can be pursued so a legitimate question is, why choose to interview? The established nature of the technique and its long history in the field means it has a number of advantages. First, there are a range of resources available to support the researcher. For example, there are numerous texts about interviewing that provide more in-depth detail on the different approaches than can be covered here. So, there are a range of places the prospective interviewer can go to learn more about the technique. Second, there will be numerous examples of dissertations based on interview research in your university library and a consider-able volume of published research based on interview studies, some of which have been highlighted in earlier chapters. Third, as stated right at the start of this book, most of us are familiar with the term interview and with what the expectations sur-rounding an interview are, so when recruiting participants to your study they will know what to expect. Also, as King (2004a) points out, people often like to talk about their work, so there is the chance that interviewees will enjoy the experience of being interviewed which again will make them more willing to participate in your study.

A fourth advantage which we have returned to time and time again in the earlier chapters is that the interview is a very flexible technique which can be used for a variety of different research questions and within a variety of epistemological posi-tions. It can also be used in both structured and unstructured formats and with both qualitative and quantitative forms of analysis. So, we could say that the interview has something to offer everybody. Finally, from my own experience, I would say that if you are interested in a particular organizational phenomenon and are keen to find out how people experience it, then there is nothing better than asking them about it directly, and the interview enables us to do that.

Disadvantages of the research interview

Having outlined the advantages, we now summarize the disadvantages. Above all, the main disadvantage of an interview study is its time-consuming nature. Throughout the whole plan, there are places where there can be hold-ups in the research process. Finding people to participate in an interview study can take a long time in that you are asking them for a considerable time commitment. Once the interviews are conducted, transcribing the data always takes longer than expected and the sheer volume of data generated by the in-depth interview process can be daunting for dissertation researchers who may be conducting interviews for the first time. Given the time-bound nature of the graduate dissertation, these are important factors to consider.

Other disadvantages focus on the nature of the data collected. In some areas in the business and management field, research based on interviews, because of the small sample sizes, is seen to have less status or credibility than research based on surveys and quantitative analysis. Although Buchanan and Bryman (2007) suggest that the field is no longer constrained by positivist approaches with their resultant emphasis on quantitative techniques, this is an issue that different areas of the business and management arena – and indeed different supervisors – will have somewhat different views about. When thinking about how to defend the methodology of your research, it is useful to consider the different criteria through which research is evaluated and how your research project overall delivers on those criteria (Johnson et al., 2006). My own view is that dissertations based on interview studies can produce excellent and useful research outcomes, though other commentators may differ.

Finally, in summing up both, I would suggest that the advantages associated with the quality data that interviews can provide far outweigh the disadvantages outlined above. Conducting a graduate dissertation is always rife with difficulties as well as joys, and there is no guarantee that choosing one research method over another will produce a smoother dissertation experience. What really matters is choosing the method that you think will best address your research question.

What makes a good interview?

Within earlier chapters, I have sought to provide guidance about conducting 'good interviews' that produce 'high quality' research data. It is usually the case that the quality of the interview is typically linked to the quality of the data collected. There are also quality issues surrounding the interview process, and, as Alvesson (2003: 17) suggests, the effective use of the interview, as defined in most texts on the subject, is related to 'how to get the interview subject to talk a lot – openly, trustfully, honestly, clearly and freely – about what the researcher is interested in'. Whereas this has been presented in a relatively straightforward manner so far within this book, defining the quality of interview research can be problematic. Given the range of different traditions within which interview research is conducted – as discussed in Chapter 2 – a range of criteria may be needed to fairly assess the contribution of a particular study.

Quality within the area of qualitative research more generally is always difficult to define in that different readers may have different understandings of what is high quality work, whereas the criteria for assessing quantitative research are less contested (Symon and Cassell, 2006). From my own perspective, as someone who has conducted many research interviews and examined many graduate-level dissertations, what I look for is that the researcher has conducted a well-designed study and has a clear rationale for how their choice of interview methods will effectively address their research questions. I expect that the study will have been conducted in a suitably ethical manner and that the voices of the interviewees have been adequately captured and illustrated in an authentic manner throughout the dissertation. I also hope that the dissertation tells a good story from beginning to end – not that it is a piece of fiction! – but rather that there is a carefully crafted argument throughout. I am always impressed to see evidence of learning through the dissertation in that the final results may produce something not necessarily expected or predicted at the beginning.

AFTER THE INTERVIEW: THE NEXT STEPS

Once the interviews are complete, the remaining tasks for the researcher are to analyse the data and write it up in a way suitable for presentation in the dissertation. We now briefly consider each of these stages.

Preparing for data analysis

In the sections that follow, I introduce some of the different ways in which interview data can be analysed. It is important to note that the analytic methods mentioned here will be addressed in detail in other books in this series, hence the cursory treatment of them here. The framework outlined in Chapter 2 is returned to at the end of these sections on analysis as a way of indicating what influences the choice of data analysis technique. In discussing analysis, it is likely that with structured interviews the pro forma for analysis will already be designed before the interview takes place, in that the analysis is likely to be quantitative. However, there are a variety of different ways to analyse semi-structured interviews.

Semi-structured interviews – once converted into transcripts – will generally produce a considerable volume of textual data that need analysis. There are many competing arguments about the best ways to analyse qualitative data and a variety of options are available to the researcher. These arguments tie in with different debates about ontology and epistemology and the different types of interviews conducted. Some forms of data analysis, such as thematic analysis, fit in with most forms of interview and are not wedded to a particular philosophical approach. Others, such as discourse analysis, fit with a particular ontology, in this case social constructionism. Hence, there are links here between the type of interview conducted, the epistemological approach of the researcher and the type of analytic technique used.

In terms of approaching the analysis, you first need to have the interview data available in such a way that it can be effectively interrogated, and second have a strategy for that interrogation process. The key task that the analyst has is to reduce the large amount of text to produce something that is empirically and theoretically interesting. Therefore, the researcher needs to be able to work towards identifying patterns in the data and constructing conceptual frameworks.

Initial tips for data analysis

One thing that distinguishes the analysis of qualitative data from that of quantitative data is that the analyst does not need to have all the data coded before the analysis process starts. Rather, analysis can start as soon as the first interview has been transcribed. If using thematic analysis, for example, it is useful to start coding data right away. Otherwise, like transcription, this can become a large and unmanageable task if left to the end. Indeed, given the time-bound nature of the graduate dissertation, my advice is that once a couple of interviews have been conducted, ideally further interviews, transcription and analysis should all be taking place at the same time. Qualitative data analysis is an iterative process. This means that the analyst is thinking conceptually about how different pieces of data fit together from the beginning, therefore it is important that these thought processes are monitored, for example through a research diary or by the use of analytic memos or another form of notation system. Otherwise, the development of patterns and the path by which eventual findings are reached may be lost through the ongoing iterative process.

Different forms of data analysis

There are a number of different forms of qualitative data analysis that are appropriate for analysing interviews. There is not the space to address all of them here, so instead some of them are briefly mentioned so that the reader can see how different types of data analysis may fit with different types of interviews. More details on these different types of data analysis can be found in other books in this series.

One common way of analysing qualitative data is content analysis. Content analysis can be defined as 'any technique for making inferences by objectively and systematically identifying specified characteristics of messages' (Holsti, 1969: 14). This is more likely to be used for structured interview formats where the purpose is information gathering or hypothesis testing. The reason for this is that the intention of content analysis is to turn qualitative data into a format where it can be quantitatively analysed. Saunders et al. (2012) suggest that content analysis has the following procedures: selection of a research question; design of a sampling frame with a clear rationale; development of a coding scheme with a manual where all the categories and the coding process are defined; and the coding of the interview data according to the manual. Statistical analysis is then conducted on the numbers of entries under different codes. The advantages of using content analysis are that there are clear and transparent procedures and therefore opportunities for the minimization of personal bias which is important in structured interviews where we may be, for example, seeking to test hypotheses. However, some would argue that in reducing our interview data in this way we lose a lot of the richness, and the focus on counting is not appropriate for the analysis of qualitative data.

A different approach is thematic analysis: a technique for analysing data that relies on organizing textual data thematically according to a template of codes, some of which will be predefined and some of which will emerge from the process of analysis. Thematic analysis can be used in a range of epistemological traditions and is a fairly flexible technique. One of the most well-used forms of thematic analysis in the business and management field is template analysis (King, 1998, 2004b, 2012). Here, the 'researcher produces a list of codes (a template) representing themes identified in their textual data' (King, 1998: 118). Thematic analysis can be used for all kinds of semi-structured and unstructured interview formats and enables the interviewer to put a clear structure on the analysis of their study. An example of a template excerpt can be found in Box 6.1.

6.1 Example of a template

Below is an extract from the template created in order to analyse experiences of customer abuse in the taxi driver study conducted by Vicky Bishop and myself.

Customer abuse

2.1 Location and time of abuse

    2.1.1 Frequency

2.2 Responses to abuse

    2.2.1 Changes in behaviour

    2.2.2 Dealing with it at the time

    2.2.3 Family

    2.2.4 Other taxi drivers

    2.2.5 Police

    2.2.6 Switching off

2.3 Suggestions for combating abuse

2.4 Types of abuse

    2.4.1 Attacking the cab

    2.4.2 Direction disputes

    2.4.3 Not paying/doing a runner, aka bilking

    2.4.4 Other customer anti-social behaviour

    2.4.5 Racism

    2.4.6 Robbery

    2.4.7 Rudeness and stroppiness

    2.4.8 Swearing, verbal and general abuse

    2.4.9 Unexpected behaviour

    2.4.10 Violence and physical abuse

Further details about devising a template and thematic analysis more generally can be found in King and Brooks in this series. Template analysis has many advantages for the interviewer who may be approaching qualitative data analysis for the first time.

It has a relatively straightforward set of procedures, is flexible, and the structure of the template enables eventual interpretation of the data. However, in reducing the data in this way it is possible to lose a sense of the individual interviewee when you are considering parts of their data alongside that of other interviewees and outside of the overall transcript context.

One of the most well-known techniques for the analysis of qualitative data is grounded theory (Glaser and Strauss, 1967). Grounded theory is the development of theory inductively from the analysis of qualitative data. An important aspect of the approach is that the researcher does not begin with a pre-conceived theory in mind, but rather begins with a general area of study. Hence, grounded theory is particularly applicable in interview studies where there is currently little theory available so the development of new theory is appropriate. Here, the sampling strategy is theoretical sampling where the choice of who next to interview depends on who is most likely to enable theory development. The process of grounded theory focuses on developing categories that illuminate the data. Through a process of constant comparison between categories, data are entered into the relevant category. The major categories are finally integrated to form a larger theoretical scheme where theoretical saturation is achieved. The advantages of using grounded theory are that there is a comprehensive set of procedures that can be followed and it is particularly useful in areas where little theory has previously been developed. The disadvantages are that it is considerably time-consuming and there are a number of ambiguities and uncertainties that are difficult to manage in the confines of a graduate dissertation.

More recently, with the linguistic turn in management and business research in the 1980s, there has been the development of a plurality of new forms of analytic methods where the focus is on talk and language use. The key concern here is on language as social practice in its own right and on how individuals use language in specific social and cultural contexts. There are many different types of analysis that fit into this category and examples include stories and narrative (Boje, 1991, 2001; Czarniawska, 1997; Alvesson and Karreman, 2000; Gabriel, 2000; Wodak and Meyer, 2010); rhetorical analysis (Symon, 2008); conversational analysis (Greatbatch and Clark, 2012); and metaphor analysis (Cornelissen et al., 2008; Cassell and Lee, 2012). In applying these methods, the interviewer will examine in detail the talk used by the interviewees, so these approaches can be used for both semi-structured and unstructured interview formats.

Choosing an appropriate technique for analysis

Given the variety of alternative approaches available for the analysis of interview data, a key question is, how does the interviewer choose between them? A first consideration is the level of structure of the research aims – for example, is the research aiming to test hypotheses, answer research questions or explore sensitizing concepts? This fits in with the level of structure of the interviews which have produced the data. As stated earlier, if the aim is to test hypotheses then the interviewer needs as structured an interview schedule as possible and should be guided towards some form of content analysis. This ties in to another impor-tant consideration which is epistemological and ontological integrity in that the method of data analysis needs to link in with the underlying philosophical stance of the research. So, for example, discourse analysis fits with social constructionism. A third consideration which is an important one but one rarely discussed within research textbooks is the personal preferences of the interviewer. My experience of supervising graduate research projects is that some people are more comfortable with more structured techniques such as template analysis, for example, whereas others are happy with the ambiguity and complexity offered by more unstructured techniques. The individual preferences of the researcher will have earlier been dis-played through the choice of interview format, so these will surface again here. My advice to students is that they read extensively around the different techniques so that they are familiar enough with them to be able to make informed choices. Other books in this series focus on some of these different analytic methods and will be able to offer insightful accounts of the different approaches. Table 6.1 highlights how the different types of analytic techniques available link in to different forms of data analysis.

Table 6.1 Different types of data analysis for different types of interviews

Level of structure	Type of interview	Purpose of interview	Forms of data analysis
Structured	Information gathering	Gather attitude/opinion data that can be quantified for analysis	Content analysis
	Hypothesis testing	Gather data for quantification and theory testing	Content analysis
Semi-structured, thematic format	Exploratory	Gather information about a given topic	Thematic analysis/ Grounded theory
	Theoretical	Generate data to enable theory development	Thematic analysis/ Grounded theory
Semi-structured, distinctive format	Event based	Generate data through understanding how interviewees make sense of different events	Thematic analysis of events
	Comparative	Generate data through forcing the interviewee to make comparisons	Thematic analysis of constructs
	Narrative	Encourage interviewees to tell stories from their own perspective	Thematic analysis/ Linguistic forms of analysis

Level of structure	Type of interview	Purpose of interview	Forms of data analysis
	Biographical	Gain insights into the interviewee's experiences through chronological reflection	Thematic analysis/ Linguistic forms of analysis/Grounded theory
	Visual techniques	Generate data by encouraging participants to project their own views or feelings onto a visual stimulus	Thematic analysis/ Linguistic forms of analysis
Unstructured	Phenomenological	Gain insights into an individual's lifeworld	Thematic analysis/ Linguistic forms of analysis

Using CAQDAS (Computer assisted qualitative data analysis software)

There are a number of different computerized packages available to help with the analysis of qualitative data. These are useful for helping with all mechanical aspects of the data analysis process - for example, creating sets of categories or themes; allocating various chunks of data to categories; creating or merging sub-categories; and comparing segments of data. Certain packages such as NVivo also enable the researcher to keep analytic memos throughout the coding process. Within the literature on qualitative research, there has been some debate about the appropriateness of using such packages for data analysis. For example, some have asserted that software packages seem more suited to objectivist grounded theory than to more social constructivist approaches (Charmaz, 2006); whilst others have suggested that the use of such software can lead to a superficial view of qualitative research due to the over-emphasis on coding (Coffey et al., 1996). Despite these concerns, the use of such packages can be helpful in enabling the researcher to effectively organize the data. An important point to remember, however, is that the most important part of the analysis - the interpretation - still needs to be done by the researcher. The software can merely help with the organization of data.

PRESENTING INTERVIEW DATA

Writing up the findings from qualitative interviews can be particularly daunting for someone who may be new to this kind of research. Furthermore, the qualitative researcher needs to be particularly skilful in writing because, unlike quantitative work, which can be interpreted through tables and summaries, qualitative work carries its meaning in the entire text (Richardson, 2000). Excerpts from interviews can be very powerful in write-ups and should be used in the dissertation's findings section to elaborate on findings, develop arguments and illustrate the points being made. There are different ways of doing this.

One of the most important things to remember when presenting qualitative data is that it is important to analyse or interpret the data and not to just present the data. A common mistake is just to present numerous quotes or excerpts from the transcripts without explanation and therefore leave the reader to make the analytic links. Rather, the interviewer must present their own interpretation of the data presented. The key rule is to never present a list of different quotes without a commentary to illustrate how they are being used to develop the argument. Extracts from the data should always be accompanied by your own commentary. An example is shown in Box 6.2.

6.2   Example of writing up data from qualitative interviews

This extract comes from an article by Cassell and Symon (2011) where a series of interviews were conducted with work psychologists regarding their views on how good qualitative research was defined within the work psychology field. The data were analysed using narrative analysis and the extract below highlights how quotes from the transcripts can be integrated with commentary to construct an argument:

'A third alternative plot underpinning this narrative saw qualitative research as fit for purpose when it met criteria that were associated with good research more generally, rather than reliability and validity and other positivist criteria more specifically. One example here is the opportunity to contribute to theory:

'It has to be theoretically driven, theoretically based, some theoretical implications and that there was some strategy in mind when you undertook the study – whether again it's a case study, a content analysis, an in-depth interview – and it stimulated ideas.' (Journal Editor)

The quality of the writing was also identified as important:

'I guess the main thing is how well it is documented. I mean do I feel that they've really gone through the process and can I trust the description in a way? So I think in a way qualitative research is always very, very tedious. I mean if it sounds like they've done a lot of tedious work, they've probably done good qualitative research.' (Research Centre Director)

In both these extracts, it would seem that a key criterion is that the account has to be convincing enough for us to trust the researcher's version of what happened during the analytic process and the outcomes of that analytic process. It is interesting that the second extract refers to the need for researchers to have been through some 'tedious' process. It seems that one indication of trust and reassurance that the research has been conducted appropriately is the suffering of the qualitative researcher.

Source: Cassell and Symon (2011).

Extracts or quotations from your data can also be used to contextualize findings and can bring thick, vivid descriptions. There is a temptation sometimes to use quotes that you think are particularly juicy rather than thinking carefully about how a chosen transcript excerpt helps to develop the argument. It is better to use fewer choice examples; indeed, as Wolcott (2001: 134) suggests, 'Save the best and drop the rest'. When using quotes, you should also say the purpose of them, for example are they being used to illustrate points made in the interviews or are you using them in a representative way? Or are you using them to present a range of alternative views that emerged from the transcripts?

Qualitative researchers often feel constrained by the word counts of various outputs so one way of dealing with this is to present illustrative data from the interviews in tables. This can be used to helpfully summarize the argument. An example of this from a narrative interview study is shown in Box 6.3.

6.3 Presenting interview data in tables to develop the argument

The following table comes from an article written by Vicky Bishop and myself in which we presented examples of story data from interviews with employment services workers about customer abuse. The aim is to illustrate the different genres of stories and the plots identified.

Story genre	Plot	Examples of words/phrases used
Spoken	Frontliner as victim of physically violent, villainous customer	'he threatened me', 'he [said that] he will see me outside', 'he was very aggressive ... I ended up calling the security guard'
		Other examples:
		'he [the customer] came up with a knife ... I am not the only one he has attacked', 'she [the customer] said she was gonna get me when I came out of work in the evening ... I was so scared that John walked me to my car'

(Continued)

(Continued)

Story genre	Plot	Examples of words/phrases used
	Frontliner as victim of stupid and unintelligent customer	'we couldn't understand why for one minute, that we would have expected her to sit on the loo and wait for an interview', 'she was a bit bolshy and irate ... [she said that she] knelt on a drawing pin and it went septic ... I don't know how I stopped myself laughing ... d'oh'
	Frontliner as victim of unreasonable customer	'we have one particular client ... he's fallen out with everybody else in the office', 'she [the customer] was ... totally unreasonable', 'she [the customer] refused to help herself ... she refused to move'
	Frontliner as problem solver/professional helping customer as victim	'The client was confused and upset ... I explained the types of benefits there were ... without using jargon ... the client was impressed with the service we offered and left the job centre satisfied', 'Although the client was illiterate ... I went through the available options ... using the system [for a] ... satisfied customer'

CONCLUSIONS

Within this book, we have covered most of what the dissertation student needs to know about interviewing, including the different types of interviews available; how to prepare and conduct an interview; some of the complexities that may arise; the advantages and disadvantages of using interviews; and what to do once the interviews are over.

Interviewing offers many opportunities for graduate researchers to have rich experiences in conducting the research for their dissertations. I wish you all the best for the interviews that lie ahead.

REFERENCES

Alexander, C.S., Meising, A.M. and Parsons, P.L. (2005). How important are stakeholder relationships? *Academy of Strategic Management Journal*, 4: 1-7.

Alvesson, M. (2003). Beyond neopositivists, romantics, and localists: a reflexive approach to interviews in organizational research, *Academy of Management Review*, 28(1): 13-33.

Alvesson, M. (2011). *Interpreting interviews*. London: Sage.

Alvesson, M. and Ashcraft, K. (2012). Interviews. In G. Symon and C.M. Cassell (eds) *Qualitative organizational research: core methods and current challenges*. London: Sage, pp. 239-57.

Alvesson, M. and Karreman, D. (2000). Varieties of discourse: on the study of organizations through discourse analysis. *Human Relations*, 53(9): 1125-49.

Alvesson, M. and Sköldberg, K. (2000). *Reflexive methodology: new vistas for qualitative research*. London: Sage.

Alvesson, M. and Sköldberg, K. (2011). *Reflexive methodology: new vistas for qualitative research*, 2nd edition. London: Sage.

Benyon, H. (1973). *Working for Ford*. Harmondsworth: Penguin Books.

Blumrodt, J., Bryson, D. and Flanagan, J. (2012). European football teams' CSR engagement impacts on customer-based brand equity. *Journal of Consumer Marketing*, 29(7): 482-93.

Boje, D. (1991). The storytelling organization: a study of story performance in an office supply firm. *Administrative Science Quarterly*, 36: 106-26.

Boje, D. (2001). *Narrative methods for organizational and communication research*. London: Sage.

Bondy, K. and Starkey, K. (2014). The dilemmas of internationalization: corporate social responsibility in the multinational corporation. *British Journal of Management*, 25(1): 4-22.

Braunscheidel, M.B., Hamister, J.W., Suresh, M.C. and Star, H. (2010). An institutional theory perspective on Six Sigma adoption. *International Journal of Operations & Production Management*, 31(4): 423-51.

Bryman, A. and Bell, E. (2007). *Business research methods*, 2nd edition. Oxford: Oxford University Press.

Bryman, A. and Cassell, C.M. (2006). The researcher interview: a reflexive perspective. *Qualitative Research in Organizations and Management: An International Journal*, 1(1): 41-55.

Buchanan, D. and Bryman, A. (2007). Contextualising methods choice in organizational research. *Organizational Research Methods*, 10(3): 483-501.

Cassell, C.M. (2005). Creating the role of the interviewer: identity work in the management research process. *Qualitative Research*, 5(2): 167-79.

Cassell, C.M. (2008). Interviews in organizational research. In D. Buchanan and A. Bryman (eds) *The Sage handbook of organizational research methods*. London: Sage, pp. 500-15.

Cassell, C.M. and Bishop, V. (2014). Metaphors and sensemaking: understanding the taint associated with dirty work. *Qualitative Research in Organizations and Management: An Internation Journal*, 9(3): 254-69.

Cassell, C.M. and Lee, B. (2012). Driving, steering, leading and defending: journey and warfare metaphors of change agency in trade union learning initiatives. *Journal of Applied Behavioral Science*, 48(2): 248-71.

Cassell, C.M. and Symon, G. (2004). *Essential guide to qualitative methods in organizational research*. London: Sage.

Cassell, C.M. and Symon, G. (2011). Assessing 'good' qualitative research in the work psychology field: a narrative analysis. *Journal of Occupational and Organizational Psychology*, 84(4): 633-50.

Cassell, C.M. and Walsh, S. (2004). Repertory grids. In C.M. Cassell and G. Symon (eds) *Essential guide to qualitative methods in organizational research*. London: Sage, pp. 61-72.

Cassell, C.M., Nadin, S., Gray, M. and Clegg, C.W. (2002). Exploring human resource management practices in small and medium sized enterprises. *Personnel Review*, 31(6): 671-92.

Charmaz, K. (2006). *Constructing grounded theory*. Thousand Oaks, CA: Sage.

Chell, E. (2004). Critical incident technique. In C.M. Cassell and G. Symon (eds) *Essential guide to qualitative methods in organizational research*. London: Sage, pp. 45-60.

Coffey, A., Holbrook, B. and Atkinson, P. (1996). Qualitative data analysis: technologies and representations. *Sociological Research Online*, 1(1), at: http://www.socresonline.org.uk/1/1/4.html

Cohen, C. and Mallon, M. (2001). My brilliant career? Using stories as a methodological tool in careers research. *International Studies of Management and Organization*, 31(3): 48-68.

Collinson, J.A. (2006). Just 'non-academics'? Research administrators and contested occupational identity. *Work, Employment and Society*, 20(2): 267-88.

Colquitt, J.A., Conlon, D.E, Wesson, M.J., Porter, O.L.H. and Yee Ng, K. (2001). Justice at the millennium: a meta-analytic review of twenty-five years of organizational justice research. *Journal of Applied Psychology*, 86(3): 425-45.

Conti, J.A. and O'Neill, M. (2007). Studying power: qualitative methods and the global elite. *Qualitative Research*, 7(1): 63-82.

Cope, J. (2005). Researching entrepreneurship through phenomenological inquiry: philosophical and methodological issues. *International Small Business Journal*, 23: 163-89.

Corbin, J. and Strauss, A. (2008). *Basics of qualitative research: techniques and procedures for developing grounded theory*, 3rd edition. Thousand Oaks, CA: Sage.

Cornelissen, J.P., Oswick, C., Christensen, A.T. and Phillips, N. (2008). Metaphor in organizational research: context, modalities and implications for research. *Organization Science*, 29(1): 7-22.

Czarniawska, B. (1997). *Narrating the organization: dramas of institutional identity.* Chicago: University of Chicago Press.

Dalton, M. (1959). *Men who manage: fusions of feeling and theory in administration.* New York: John Wiley & Sons.

Dennis, W.M. and Parkhe, A. (2002). Hungarian-Western partnerships: a grounded theoretical model of integration processes and outcomes. *Journal of International Business Studies*, 33(3): 423-55.

Denzin, N.K. (2001). The reflexive interview and a performative social science. *Qualitative Research*, 1(1): 23-46.

Denzin, N.K. and Lincoln, Y.S. (2005). Introduction: the discipline and practice of qualitative research. In N.K. Denzin and Y.S. Lincoln (eds) *The Sage handbook of qualitative research*, 3rd edition. Thousand Oaks, CA: Sage, pp. 1-32.

Donnelly, P.F., Gabriel, Y. and Özkazanç-Pan, B. (2013). Untold stories of the field. *Qualitative Research in Organizations and Management: An International Journal*, 8(1): 4-15.

Druskat, V.U. and Wheeler, J.V. (2003). Managing from the boundary: the effective leadership of self-managing work teams. *Academy of Management Journal*, 46(4): 435-57.

Duberley, J., Johnson, P. and Cassell, C.M. (2012). Philosophies underpinning qualitative research. In G. Symon and C.M. Cassell (eds) *Qualitative Organizational Research: Core Methods and Current Challenges*. London: Sage, pp. 15-34.

Duberley, J., Johnson, P., Cassell, C.M. and Close, P. (2000). Manufacturing change: the role of performance evaluation and control systems. *International Journal of Operations and Production Management*, 20(4): 427-41.

Easterby-Smith, M., Thorpe, R. and Jackson, P. (2008). *Management Research*. London: Sage.

Ekinci, Y. (2015). *Designing research questionnaires for business and management students*. London: Sage.

Flanagan, J.C. (1954). The critical incident technique. *Psychological Bulletin*, 51(4): 327-58.

Fontana, A. and Frey, J.H. (2005). The interview: from neutral stance to political involvement. In N.K. Denzin and Y.S. Lincoln (eds) *The Sage handbook of qualitative research*, 3rd edition. Thousand Oaks, CA: Sage, pp. 695-728.

Gabriel, Y. (2000). *Storytelling in organizations: facts, figures and fantasies*. New York: Oxford University Press.

Gabriel, Y. and Griffiths, D.S. (2004). Stories in organizational research. In C.M. Cassell and G. Symon (eds) *Essential guide to qualitative methods in organizational research*. London: Sage, pp. 114–26.

Gammack, J.G. and Stephens, R.A. (1994). Repertory grid in constructive interaction. In C.M. Cassell and G. Symon (eds) *Qualitative methods in organizational research: a practical guide*. London: Sage, pp. 72–90.

Gendron, Y. and Spira, L.F. (2010). Identity narratives under threat: a study of former members of Arthur Andersen. *Accounting, Organizations and Society*, 35: 275–300.

Gill, J. and Johnson, P. (2010). *Research methods for managers*, 4th edition. London: Sage.

Glaser, B. and Strauss, A. (1967). *The discovery of grounded theory: strategies for qualitative research*. Chicago: Aldine.

Greatbatch, D. and Clark, T. (2012). Conversation analysis in management research. In G. Symon and C.M. Cassell (eds) *Qualitative organizational research: core methods and current challenges*. London: Sage, pp. 451–72.

Gremler, D.D. (2004). The critical incident technique in service research. *Journal of Service Research*, 7: 65–89.

Hahn, G.J., Hill, W.J., Hoeri, R.W. and Zinkgraf, S.A. (1999). The impact of Six Sigma improvement: a glimpse into the future of statistics. *The American Statistician*, 53: 208–15.

Hamilton, E. (2006). Narratives of enterprise as epic tragedy. *Management Decision*, 44(4): 536–50.

Hammersley, M. (1996). The relationship between qualitative and quantitative research: paradigm loyalty versus methodological eclecticism. In J.T.E. Richardson (ed.) *Handbook of research methods for psychology and the social sciences*. Leicester: BPS Books, pp. 159–74.

Hammersley, M. (2010). Reproducing or constructing? Some questions about transcription in social research. *Qualitative Research*, 10(5): 553–69.

Hanna, P. (2012). Using internet technologies (such as Skype) as a research medium: a research note. *Qualitative Research*, 12(2): 239–42.

Harvey, W.S. (2011). Strategies for conducting elite interviews. *Qualitative Research*, 11(4): 431–51.

Hayes, T. and Mattimoe, R. (2004). To tape or not to tape: reflections on methods of data collection. In C. Humphrey and B. Lee (eds) *The real life guide to accounting research: a behind-the-scenes view of using qualitative research methods*. Amsterdam: Elsevier, pp. 359–72.

Haynes, K. (2006). A therapeutic journey: reflections on the effects of research on researcher and participants. *Qualitative Research in Organizations and Management: An International Journal*, 1(3): 204–21.

Haynes, K. (2012). Reflexivity in qualitative research. In G. Symon and C.M. Cassell (eds) *Qualitative organizational research: core methods and current challenges*. London: Sage, pp. 72–89.

Head, E. (2009). The ethics and implications of paying participants in qualitative research. *International Journal of Social Research Methodology*, 12(4):
1464-5300.

Herzog, H. (2005). On home turf: interview location and its social meaning. *Qualitative Sociology*, 28(1): 25-47.

Hollway, W. (1991). *Work psychology and organizational behaviour: managing the individual at work*. London: Sage.

Holstein, J. and Gubrium, J. (1995). *The active interview.* Thousand Oaks, CA: Sage.

Holsti, O.R. (1969). *Content analysis for the social sciences and humanities*. Reading: Addison-Wesley.

Holt, A. (2010). Using the telephone for narrative interviewing: a research note. *Qualitative Research*, 10(1): 113-21.

Holt, R. (2012). Ethical research practice. In G. Symon and C.M. Cassell (eds) *Qualitative organizational research: core methods and current challenges*. London: Sage, pp. 90-108.

Jahoda, M., Lazarsfeld, P.F. and Zeisel, H. (1972). *Marienthal: the sociography of an unemployed community.* London: Tavistock Publications.

James, N. and Busher, H. (2006). Credibility, authenticity and voice: dilemmas in online interviewing. *Qualitative Research*, 6: 403-20.

Johnson, J., Bristow, D.N., McClure, D.J. and Schneider, K.C. (2011). Determinants of job satisfaction among long-distance truck drivers: an interview study in the United States. *International Journal of Management*, 28(1/2): 203-16.

Johnson, P. and Duberley, J. (2003). Reflexivity in management research. *Journal of Management Studies*, 40(5): 1279-303.

Johnson, P., Buehring, A., Cassell, C.M. and Symon, G. (2006). Evaluating qualitative management research: towards a contingent criteriology. *International Journal of Management Reviews*, 8(3): 131-56.

Jowett, A., Peel, E. and Shaw, R. (2011). On-line interviewing in psychology: reflections on the process. *Qualitative Research in Psychology*, 8: 354-69.

Kamla, R. (2012). Syrian women accountants' attitudes and experiences at work in the context of globalization. *Accounting, Organizations and Society*, 37: 188-205.

Kelan, E.K. and Mah, A. (2014). Gendered identification: between idealization and admiration. *British Journal of Management*, 21(1): 91-101.

Kelly, G.A. (1955). *The psychology of personal constructs: volumes 1 and 2*. New York: Norton.

Kezar, A. (2003). Transformational elite interviews: principles and problems. *Qualitative Inquiry*, 9(3): 395-415.

King, N. (1998). Template analysis. In G. Symon and C.M. Cassell (eds) *Qualitative methods and analysis in organizational research*. London: Sage, pp. 118-34.

King, N. (2004a). Using interviews in qualitative research. In C.M. Cassell and G. Symon (eds) *Essential guide to qualitative methods in organizational research*. London: Sage, pp. 11-22.

King, N. (2004b). Using templates in the thematic analysis of text. In C.M. Cassell and G. Symon (eds) *Essential guide to qualitative methods in organizational research.* London: Sage, pp. 256–70.

King, N. (2012). Doing template analysis. In G. Symon and C.M. Cassell (eds) *Qualitative organizational research: core methods and current challenges.* London: Sage, pp. 426–50.

King, N. and Horrocks, C. (2010). *Interviews in qualitative research.* London: Sage.

Kvale, S. (2006). Dominance through interviews and dialogues. *Qualitative Inquiry,* 12: 480–500.

Langan-Fox, J. and Tan, P. (1997). Images of a culture in transition: personal constructs of organizational stability and change. *Journal of Occupational and Organizational Psychology,* 70(3): 273–93.

Lawthom, R. (1998). What do I do? A feminist in non-feminist research. *Feminism and Psychology,* 7(4): 641–52.

Learmonth, M. (2006). Doing critical management research interviews after reading Derrida. *Qualitative Research in Organizations and Management: An International Journal,* 1(2): 83–97.

Limerick, B. and O'Leary, J. (2006). Re-inventing or recycling? Examples of feminist qualitative research informing the management field. *Qualitative Research in Organizations and Management: An International Journal,* 1(2): 98–112.

Mallett, O. and Wapshott, R. (2014). Informality and employment relationship in small firms: humour, ambiguity and straight-talking. *British Journal of Management,* 25(1): 118–32.

Mayo, E. (1945). *Social problems of an industrial civilization.* Boston: Division of Research, Graduate School of Business Administration, Harvard University.

Mazzetti, A. and Blenkinsopp, J. (2012). Evaluating a visual timeline methodology for appraisal and coping. *Journal of Occupational and Organizational Psychology,* 85(4): 649–65.

McCabe, D. (2007). Individualization at work? Subjectivity, teamworking and anti-unionism. *Organization,* 14(2): 243–66.

McNamee, P. and McHugh, M. (1989). Competitive strategies in the clothing industry. *Long Range Planning,* 22(4): 63–71.

Mirchandani, K. (2003). Challenging racial silences in studies of emotion work: contributions from anti-racist feminist theory. *Organization Studies,* 24(5): 721–42.

Morgan, C.D. and Murray, H.A. (1935). A method of investigating fantasies: the Thematic Apperception Test. *Archives of Neurology and Psychiatry,* 34: 289–306.

Morgan, S. and Symon, G. (2004). Electronic interviews in organizational research. In C.M. Cassell and G. Symon (eds) *Essential guide to qualitative methods in organizational research.* London: Sage, pp. 23–33.

Musson, G. (2004). Life histories. In C.M. Cassell and G. Symon (eds) *Essential guide to qualitative methods in organizational research.* London: Sage, pp. 34–44.

Nadin, S. and Cassell, C.M. (2006). Increasing reflexivity through the use of research diaries. *Qualitative Research in Accounting and Management,* 3: 208–17.

Nairn, K., Munro, J. and Smith, A.B. (2005). A counter-narrative of a failed interview. *Qualitative Research*, 5(2): 221–44.

Oliver, D.G., Serovich, J.M. and Mason, T.L. (2005). Constraints and opportunities with interview transcription: towards reflection in qualitative research. *Social Forces*, 85(2): 1273–89.

Patton, M.Q. (2002). *Qualitative research and evaluation methods*, 3rd edition. Thousand Oaks, CA: Sage.

Paul, J. and Rana, J. (2013). Consumer behavior and purchase intention for organic food. *Journal of Consumer Marketing*, 29(6): 412–22.

Pillow, W. (2003). Confession, catharsis or cure? Rethinking the uses of reflexivity as methodological power in qualitative research. *Qualitative Studies in Education*, 16(2): 175–96.

Rapley, T.R. (2001). The art(fullness) of open-ended interviewing: some considerations on analysing interviews. *Qualitative Research*, 1(3): 303–23.

Richardson, L. (2000). Writing: a method of inquiry. In N. Denzin and Lincoln, Y. (eds) *The Handbook of Qualitative Research*, 2nd edition. Thousand Oaks, California: Sage, pp. 923–48.

Ritchie, J. and Lewis, J. (2003). *Qualitative research practice: a guide for social science students and researchers*. London: Sage.

Roberts, J. (2002). Building the complementary board: the work of the plc chairman. *Long Range Planning*, 35: 493–520.

Rorschach, H. (1942). *Psychodiagnostics: a diagnostic test based on perception*. Bern, Switzerland: Hans Huber. (Original work published in 1921.)

Saunders, M.N.K. (2012). Choosing research participants. In G. Symon and C.M. Cassell (eds) *Qualitative organizational research: core methods and current challenges*. London: Sage, pp. 35–52.

Saunders, M., Lewis, P. and Thornhill, A. (2012). *Research methods for business students*, 6th edition. Harlow: FT Prentice-Hall.

Shaw, S. and Cassell, C.M. (2007). 'That's not how I see it': female and male perspectives on the academic role. *Women in Management Review*, 22(6): 497–515.

Silverman, D. (2006). *Interpreting qualitative data: methods for analysing talk, text and interaction*, 3rd edition. London: Sage.

Slutskaya, N., Simpson, A. and Hughes, J. (2012). Lessons from photoelicitation: encouraging working men to speak. *Qualitative Research in Organizations and Management: An International Journal*, 7(1): 16–33.

Speakman, J.I.F. and Ryals, L. (2012). Key account management: the inside selling job. *Journal of Business and Industrial Marketing*, 27(5): 360–9.

Stephens, N. (2007). Collecting data from elites and ultra elites: telephone and face-to-face interviews with macroeconomists. *Qualitative Research*, 7(2): 203–16.

Steyaert, C. and Bouwen, R. (2004). Group methods of organizational analysis. In C.M. Cassell and G. Symon (eds) *Essential guide to qualitative methods in organizational research*. London: Sage, pp. 140–53.

Stiles, D. (2004). Pictorial representation. In C.M. Cassell and G. Symon (eds) *Essential guide to qualitative methods in organizational research*. London: Sage, pp. 127–39.

Sturges, J.E. and Hanrahan, K.J. (2004). Comparing telephone and face-to-face quali-
    tative interviewing. *Qualitative Research*, 4(1): 107–18.

Sveningsson, S. and Alvesson, M. (2003). Managing managerial identities: organiza-
    tional fragmentation, discourse and identity struggle. *Human Relations*, 56(10):
    1163–93.

Symon, G. (2008). Rhetoric. In R. Thorpe and R. Holt (eds) *The Sage dictionary of
    qualitative management research*. London: Sage.

Symon, G. and Cassell, C.M. (2006). Neglected perspectives in work and organiza-
    tional psychology. *Journal of Occupational and Organizational Psychology*, 79(3):
    307–14.

Tanggaard, L. (2007). The research interview as discourses crossing swords: the
    researcher and apprentice on crossing roads. *Qualitative Inquiry*, 13(1): 160–76.

Temple, B. and Young, A. (2004). Qualitative research and translation dilemmas.
    Qualitative Research, 4(2): 161–78.

Tietze, S. (2012). Researching your own organization. In G. Symon and C.M. Cassell
    (eds) *Qualitative organizational research: core methods and current challenges*.
    London: Sage, pp. 53–71.

Vaara, E. (2002). On the discursive construction of success/failure in narrative of
    post-merger integration. *Organization Studies*, 23: 211–48.

Vince, R. and Warren, S. (2012). Participatory visual methods. In G. Symon and
    C.M. Cassell (eds) *Qualitative organizational research: core methods and current
    challenges*. London: Sage, pp. 275–95.

Weick, K. (1995). *Sensemaking in organizations*. Thousand Oaks, CA: Sage.

Willman, P., Fenton-O'Creevy, M., Nicholson, N. and Soane, E. (2006). Noise trading and
    the management of operational risk. *Journal of Management Studies*, 43(6): 1357–74.

Wodak, R. and Meyer, M. (2010). *Methods of critical discourse analysis*. London: Sage.

Wolcott, H. (2001). *Writing up qualitative research*, 2nd edition. Thousand Oaks, CA:
    Sage.

Xian, H. (2008). Lost in translation? Language, culture and the roles of translator in
    cross-cultural management research. *Qualitative Research in Organizations and
    Management: An International Journal*, 3(3): 231–45.

Yin, R.K. (1994). *Case Study Research: design and methods*, 3rd edition. Thousand
    Oaks, California: Sage.

Ylijoki, O. (2005). Academic nostalgia: a narrative approach to academic work. *Human
    Relations*, 58(5): 555–76.

Zhang, D.D. and Swanson, L.A. (2013). Social entrepreneurship in nonprofit organ-
    izations: an empirical investigation of the synergy between social and business
    objectives. *Journal of Nonprofit & Public Sector Marketing*, 25(1): 105–25.

Zuckerman, H. (1972). Interviewing an ultra-elite. *The Public Opinion Quarterly*, 36(2):
    159–75.

INDEX

Fold a Frog

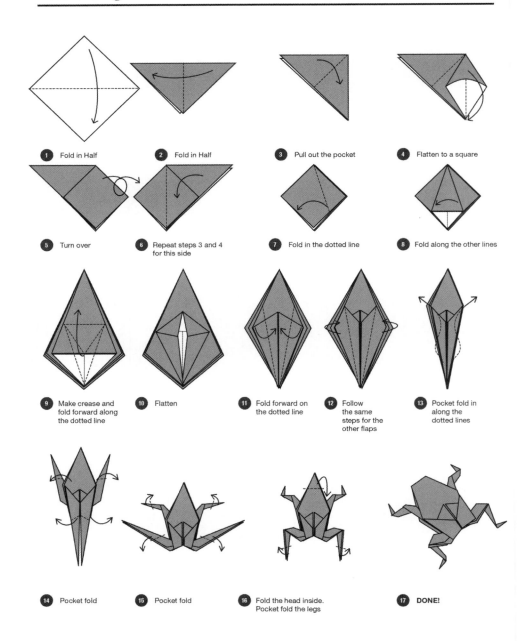

1. Fold in Half
2. Fold in Half
3. Pull out the pocket
4. Flatten to a square
5. Turn over
6. Repeat steps 3 and 4 for this side
7. Fold in the dotted line
8. Fold along the other lines
9. Make crease and fold forward along the dotted line
10. Flatten
11. Fold forward on the dotted line
12. Follow the same steps for the other flaps
13. Pocket fold in along the dotted lines
14. Pocket fold
15. Pocket fold
16. Fold the head inside. Pocket fold the legs
17. DONE!